STARS that PAUSE

EMPRESS WU BOOKS

Stars that Pause

--- ∞ ---

2,000 Years of Asian UFO Encounters & Lore

YI IZZY YU
JOHN YU BRANSCUM

Copyright © 2025 by Yi Izzy Yu and John Yu Branscum

All rights reserved.

No part of this book may be reproduced in any form or by any electronic or mechanical means, including information storage and retrieval systems, without written permission from the authors, except for the use of brief quotations in a book review.

Published by Empress Wu Books

Library of Congress Control Number: 2025920127

ISBN 978-1-953124-05-0 (pbk)

ISBN 978-1-953124-07-4 (ebook)

Cover: Based on *Meditation in a Cave* by Ren Yu (1853–1901), designed by Yiru Zhao

PRAISE FOR STARS THAT PAUSE

"A book many forteans and ufologists have longed for: a fresh, provocative, and well-argued analysis of two millennia of Asian anomalous encounters." —*Fortean Times*

"In this luminous and fascinating volume, authors Yi Izzy Yu and John Yu Branscum bring together translated ancient and contemporary accounts and refract them through Asian experience and thought. Whether ultimate explanations lie in collective madness, alien encounters, or something else entirely, *Stars That Pause* invites readers to explore all possibilities while blending paranormal, psychological, and personal interpretations in the authors' pensive and poetic style. Enigmatic and utterly absorbing." —**Lee Murray, five-time Bram Stoker Award-winner, recipient of New Zealand's Prime Minister's Award for Literary Achievement in Fiction, and co-editor of *Unquiet Spirits: Essays by Asian Women in Horror***

"An extraordinary, genre-slipping, genre-defying work that's unlike any other 'UFO' book out there. It's a historical excavation of anomalous phenomena, Asian culture and thought, and a meditation on the strange and on human perception. Along the way, it also becomes a book about philosophy, science, psychology, myth, and belief. I recommend it for those interested in UFOs and related phenomena. I also recommend it for those who scoff and think they *aren't* interested in such things. Tanta-

lizingly strange, erudite, eclectic, whimsical, and enthralling."
—**Vanessa Fogg, author of** *The House of Illusionists*

"Yu and Branscum have unearthed something most of us never knew was lost—two millennia of Asian encounters with phenomena that challenge everything we think we understand about reality. Not just another UFO book, this is a masterwork of comparative mythology and post-disclosure humanities that, like the best art, makes you see differently." —**Bil Brown, editor of** *Black & Grey* **magazine**

"*Stars That Pause* is the most ambitious and mind-bending book about UFOs I've ever read. It's mind-bending Asian science fiction that just happens to be nonfiction. Drs. Yu and Branscum's meticulous translations transport you to strange places, revealing Chinese immortals who mirror today's alien profiles, sexual encounters with non-human entities, and Taoist UFO theories rooted in qi dynamics. If you thought UFOs were a solely Western obsession, prepare to have your mind blown."
—**Xiuping Shang, poet and visual artist**

"*Stars That Pause* is a beautifully woven quilt of accounts of the unexplained and shared experiences of the strange [. . .] illuminating an intersection of worlds and realities that are more commonplace than many of us might first believe."—**Ai Jiang, Bram Stoker, Nebula, and Ignyte Award winner and author of** *A Palace Near the Wind*, *Linghun*, **and** *I AM AI*

*For Francesca Branscum, Vivianne Tabbutt, and 赵羿如.
We hope these thoughts on the strange cast light on the paths in front of you.*

The mind of the beginner is empty, free of the habits of the expert, ready to accept, to doubt, and open to all the possibilities.

—Shunryu Suzuki, *Zen Mind, Beginner's Mind*

CONTENTS

How to Read This Book — xiii

PART I
SIGHTINGS

ANCIENT CASES ANALYZED IN DISCUSSION	3
Ships Like Shells	4
Waiting for an Encounter	5
Stars That Pause	7
The Wheel	8
The Top	9
The Bird with Wheel-Like Wings I	10
The Bird with Wheel-Like Wings II	11
An Object in the Woods	12
Red Flames in Flight	13
Guests from the Sky	15
ADDITIONAL CHINESE HISTORICAL RECORDS	18
CONTEMPORARY ASIAN REPORTS	21

PART II
DISCUSSION

ANCIENT ACCOUNTS AND MODERN PARALLELS	57

PART III
RABBIT HOLES

1. EXTRAORDINARY CLAIMS AND BOGGLE THRESHOLDS	77
2. CHINESE UFO THEORY	81
3. UFOS, UAPS, AND WTFS: THE MAGIC OF NAMES	89
4. THE TAO OF JUNG	93
5. CONFESSIONS OF WILD GODS	99
6. ULTRATERRESTRIALS	103
7. THE SHADOW BOOK OF JI YUN	109

8. CURRENTLY SCREENING: MASS SIGHTINGS OF UFOS AT THE MOVIE THEATERS	111
9. IT WAS A DARK AND STORMY NIGHT: WEATHER AND THE ANOMALOUS	114
10. ATOMIC SPECIAL ATTRACTIONS: UAP INTERACTIONS WITH NUCLEAR FACILITIES	118
11. WHITE SPACE: MANGA, MANHUA, AND ANOMALOUS ENCOUNTERS	123
12. SKEPTICISM AND GASLIGHTING	127
13. COSMIC EGGS	132
14. THE SHAPES OF THINGS: UAP TRANSFORMATIONS IN EASTERN AND WESTERN ACCOUNTS	137
15. ASIAN IMMORTALS, FAIRIES, AND OTHER TRICKSTERS OF THE LIGHT	141
16. THAT'S AMORE: A GLOBAL HISTORY OF SEXUAL ENCOUNTERS WITH NON-HUMAN ENTITIES	151
17. SHAMANS AND ALIENS	161
18. SYMBOLIC THOUGHT, METAPHYSICAL QR CODES, AND UFOS	167
19. MULTI-STORIED HOUSES: MYTHOLOGICAL ENGINEERING AND UAPS	177
READER'S GUIDE: DISCUSSION QUESTIONS	189
Afterword	203
Selected Bibliography	205
Acknowledgments	223
About the Authors	225

HOW TO READ THIS BOOK

We stumbled into the world of Asian UFOs while translating Chinese historical accounts about anomalous experiences and discovering an 18th-century UFO abduction report ("Guests from the Sky") involving leading Qing dynasty political figures. This unexpected find led us to search for similar ancient accounts, as well as collect modern Asian ones, resulting in this book.

We're still not entirely sure what to make of it all. But we're certain these accounts challenge many of our neat categories: blurring lines between modern and ancient, East and West, and folklore and reportage.

This book unfolds a bit differently from most. The first section, "Sightings," presents translated accounts of ancient Chinese UFO sightings spanning nearly two millennia, as well as modern accounts across Asia. We present the raw accounts first so readers can sample and formulate their own ideas before we step in with ours.

The second section, "Discussion," unpacks the significance of ancient UFO accounts in the context of recent UAP research and modern encounters. This is a great place to start if you're a reader who likes to begin with an orienting overview first or are new to this topic. Throughout this section, you'll spot bracketed numbers, such as [5], next to certain references. Think of them as invitations to investigate our third section, "Rabbit Holes"—a collection of, well, rabbit holes that we couldn't resist falling down. In them, we dig deep into everything from Carl Jung's Taoist-influenced take on UFOs and a cross-cultural history of sexual encounters with non-human entities to Chinese UFO theory, global fairy lore, Asian shamanism, and deathbed confessions from military officials about non-human technology. These pieces are essentially small topical chapters that not only engage with some of the topics that arise in the "Discussion" section but also reflect those magical moments in our literature seminars when class conversations suddenly veer into rich, unexpected terrain.

Read this book however you like: witness some ancient and modern sightings first, or start with the orienting "Discussion" section, or dive into some interesting-looking rabbit holes before you do anything else, or flip back and forth. We've designed this structure to let you follow your curiosity wherever it takes you.

Whatever path you choose, we hope you enjoy the journey as much as we enjoyed writing this book.

And don't be surprised if you lose track of time—and look up from these accounts to find it's suddenly dark outside and full of strange lights.

PART I
SIGHTINGS

ANCIENT CASES
ANALYZED IN DISCUSSION

Ships Like Shells

At Luo River, two spiral shell-like objects as big as hills would periodically emerge from the water—light blazing from their tops so brightly that the sky would light up even during the day. These curiosities were capable of incredible speed and could cover 31 miles in a flash. Whenever these objects appeared, the weather would turn stormy.

—*Cixi County Chronicles, Records of Anomalies,* 1899

Waiting for an Encounter

Between the years of 1056 and 1063, a flying object—round and shiny like a pearl—came to Yangzhou City and was seen by many. It flew at night and retreated to local waters during day. First at Tianchang County Marsh and later in both Pishe and Xinkai Lake.

My friend's summer house bordered Pishe Lake. One evening, the object rose from the water and drifted toward him. When close, its outer shell opened and a horizontal ray of light shot out, pulsing from gold to silver white—so dazzling that my friend could only look at it from the corner of his eyes.

A chamber lay inside the opened shell. It held a floating orb the size of a fist. It was the source of the light, which now fully exposed became even more intense so that it illuminated several miles of forest like daylight and made the sky glow as if the forest were aflame. All of a sudden, the object sealed shut and darted across the lake at incredible speed.

Ancient records describe similar flying objects. They too were round and seamless. But their light is described as dimmer than what the Yangzhou City witnesses described—more like the moon's than a sun's. One exception here is "Light Pearl Fu," a poem by historian Cui Boyi of nearby Gaoyou, who likely witnessed the same phenomenon as my friend.

One last note that I should add is that the Yanzhou City flying object hasn't appeared for several years now. No one knows where it went. Still, at night people come to sleep on boats in the lake near my friend's home, hoping for their own encounter. Thus, the name given to the pavilion that borders the lake: the "Waiting for the Pearl" Pavilion.

—*Dream Pool Essays*, c. 1088

Stars That Pause

On the night of March 6, 905, a large star appeared in the middle of the sky, resembling a 50-liter vat. Its top glowed with a dazzling yellowish-red light, and above it glittered smaller lights, like a field of stars, extending some 16 meters. These smaller lights moved in sync with the main object steadily northwest, until the entire formation halted in midair, roughly 33 meters above the ground. From this still position, everything suddenly reversed direction and darted away in a zigzag motion toward the southeast. Abruptly, both the large object and the smaller stars vanished, leaving behind an immense patch of pale white vapor in the night sky, like the hazy fog that drifts through a bamboo forest.

—*New Book of Tang, Astronomical Records*, c. 1044–1060

The Wheel

On July 23, 1818, an enormous, armored wheel—black in the middle and covered with lights on the outside surface—appeared in the southeastern sky during a storm. It flew northwest with a whirling motion that made front and back indistinguishable.

More than ten families witnessed the event. They reported that the wheel made a sound like thunder as it passed. When it flew close to the ground, it pulled roof tiles, dirt, and whole trees into the air.

The incident caused great damage to the town.

—*Shanghai Songjiang Prefecture Chronicles Sequel*, 1885

The Top

In the late evening of June 24, 1561, a small yellowish-white object appeared in the northwestern sky and slowly descended. The top was pointy, and it had a broad, purple-and-red base.

As the object neared the ground, it swelled to ten times its original size, shooting brilliant rays of light in all directions that pulsed violently. When it reached the ground, it made no sound.

—*Zhenhai County Chronicles, Records of Anomalies*, 1879

The Bird with Wheel-Like Wings I

In the year of 1573, a gigantic bird-shaped thing came from the east, from the direction of Haiyan County. It was as large as a sailing ship and had wheel-shaped wings. When it raised its head and turned its tail during flight, the air grew hazy and misty, and storms erupted around it.

—Jiaxing Prefecture Chronicles, 1721

The Bird with Wheel-Like Wings II

In the year of 1575, a giant bird came from the south of the sea. It was as big as a ship and had wheel-like wings.

—*Pinghu County Chronicles, Records of Anomalies,* 1790

An Object in the Woods

On May 8, 1880, Tan, a peasant who lives in Xiyanju, went for a walk one morning in the woods behind his house. There he encountered a small floating object radiating bright, multicolored light. When he reached for it, his feet suddenly left the ground. To his terror, he floated up so high that he could hear wind whistling past.

He was in a strange state this whole time, his mind thick and hazy and his body paralyzed. He could only feel panic as, abruptly, he began to fall.

The next thing he knew, he was crashing through foliage on a mountainside—in a completely different province.

Back on the ground, he came out of his trance, feeling as though he'd just awakened from a dream. He was extremely shocked and frightened to find himself in an unfamiliar place. After a while, a woodcutter passed by and, seeing Tan was upset, asked where he was from.

Tan said, "I am from Songzi, Hubei Province."

The woodcutter exclaimed, "But this is Guizhou Province—more than a thousand li from your home!"

With the woodcutter's guidance, Tan descended the mountain. He spent 18 days walking home, begging for food along the way. The nature of the strange object he encountered remains a mystery. How strange!

—*Songzi County Chronicles*, c. 1880

Red Flames in Flight

At 8 o'clock on the night of September 28, 1892, a fireball suddenly appeared in the sky south of Nanjing City. Resembling a gigantic egg, the bright red object seemed illuminated from within and cast no light on its surroundings. Clearly visible in the dusk sky, hundreds of people gathered on Red Sparrow Bridge, gazing up and tiptoeing to get a closer look, as it drifted slowly from west to east through the clouds. The object lingered for about a meal's time before slowly fading away into the distance.

Some people said it could be a meteor, but a meteor would move fast and vanish in a flash. The egg, by contrast, moved slowly. Others proposed it could have been a sky lantern released by children, but this explanation also failed: while a strong wind was blowing northward that night, the object traveled steadily eastward.

Among the speculating crowd was an elderly man. He said, "The object made a faint sound when it first appeared and seemed to jump an incredible distance into the sky above us from the direction of the South Gate. Quite odd."

—*Red Flame in Flight* by Wu Youru, published in *Dianshizhai Pictorial*, 1892

Guests from the Sky

One day I received a letter that was written in my language but seemed to be written in a foreign one. The thoughts it expressed were odd, confused, and almost impossible to decipher. The letter's poor quality especially surprised me since my friend Shen Tiechan, who was highly intelligent and highly articulate, had written it. The letter was disturbing too because its tone was nostalgic and sorrowful, as if it was written as a final goodbye—this even though I knew that Tiechan had just begun a probationary post in Shanxi.

Not long after that, I received word that there would be no more letters. Tiechan was dead.

Life is filled with strange happenings that are hard to fit into our understanding of the world. Many we let pass in order to get on with our days. But this was not something I could let pass. I talked to Tiechan's neighbors and his friends, his family members and his enemies. Slowly, I pieced together what had pushed my friend to his tragic end. This is what I discovered.

That summer, Tiechan went hunting in the Xian mountains to restore his spirits after a long illness. The hunting trip proceeded unremarkably, with one notable exception: something followed him out of the woods.

This something took the form of two orbs in the sky, turning like windmills. No one else could see the orbs. Even Tiechan didn't see them in the way that one normally sees, which is to say that he could see them when he looked up even if his eyes were closed.

For several days, the orbs silently followed. Then suddenly, without warning, they broke open. From inside two young women emerged, floated down, and delivered a message. Their mistress, a xian nü immortal, wished to meet Tiechan.

Knowing that he could not reject such an invitation, Tiechan agreed to meet the xian nü. Instantaneously, he was transported to a room. It was unlike any he had ever been in. Its dimensions were dizzying, and its massive jade walls were eccentrically decorated with odd purple seashells. The room's strangeness made Tiechan tremble, but its effect paled compared to the appearance of the xian nü mistress. She was beautiful, yes. But it was not a peaceful kind of beauty. It was the kind of beauty that disturbs because it exceeds limits.

Her words exceeded limits as well. Shocking Tiechan, the xian nü asked him to become her lover.

When he refused, saying that he felt too overwhelmed by his strange surroundings to comply, the xian nü became angry and waved him away. The next thing he knew he was waking up on the road where the xian nü's servants first approached him.

Tiechan hoped that was the end of the matter. But several weeks later, the two rotating spheres reappeared. So did the two female servants. They did not ask him to come with them this time. They just took him. But they took him to a new place—smaller, homier, less exotic in furnishing and colors. It was much easier on his mind. So, when the xian nü asked Tiechan if he felt more comfortable now, he had no choice but to say yes. This pleased her, and she declared he then no longer had any reason to reject her. He agreed.

From then on, they met regularly—during both waking and dreaming states. "Tell no one," said the xian nü.

Tiechan promised not to and didn't for a long time—not even when he got sick. But, finally, the severity of his illness convinced him to visit a doctor who specialized in matters of both the spirit and the body. However, it was too late. Tiechan couldn't keep the red pills the doctor prescribed down, nor anything else. Everything was vomited back up. He died during one of these vomiting fits, and his last letter to me was written during these weeks of illness.

I will not forget Shen Tiechan. His qualities were simply too admirable. He wrote poetry that moved the heart and opened the mind. His calligraphy dazzled. He was witty, fun, and generous. However, no one is without secrets or vices, and I discovered one more fact about Tiechan during my investigation—one that might provide a clue to how all the weird events began.

In Tiechan's middle age, he had begun to mourn the passing of his youthful looks and obsess about death. This launched his pursuit of a formula for immortality. He acquired books of occult knowledge and sought out alchemists and sorcerers who were rumored to dabble in forbidden magic. It is no surprise then that something inexplicable occurred that ultimately led to his death. However, it is a shame. While spiritual entities of many kinds exist, they usually won't molest human beings unless a person goes out of their way to make themselves known. Through my investigations, it seems to me that the manifestations of such entities, and the tragedies that follow in their wake, are prompted not by events in the external world but mysteriously conjured by events in one's internal world: the desires of the heart and what one dares imagine. If only Tiechan had guarded these inner borders better.

—Originally published in 1800 in *Yuewei Caotang Biji*; Translated in *The Shadow Book of Ji Yun*, 2021

ADDITIONAL CHINESE HISTORICAL RECORDS

During the morning hours on January 1, 314, the sun descended to the ground. Then three suns appeared in the west, one after another, and steadily traveled east.

—The Book of Jin, Chronicle of Emperor Min, 648

In January 814, a big star—approximately half the size of a mat—was seen ascending from the ground into the night sky, its radiance illuminating the land below. A multitude of smaller stars followed it.

—New Book of Tang, Astronomical Records, c. 1044–1060

In December 906, a star resembling Venus appeared at dusk in the east. It rose slowly upward from the horizon to mid-sky and shone like a waxing crescent moon. Then it swerved from its original path, and shortly afterwards, it split into two.

—*New Book of Tang, Astronomical Records*, c. 1044–1060

On June 4, 969, a star emerged from the Hegu constellation, moved slowly across the sky and then slowly descended, its light illuminating the ground.

—*History of Song, Astronomical Records*, 1345

On the night of August 15, 1167, the sky was cloudy with only dim moonlight visible. A wheel-shaped object, about half the width of the moon, appeared in the sky. The wheel then broke apart, dispersing into what seemed like hundreds of thousands of tiny stars. The jade-green auroras in the sky emitted indescribable, dazzling light. Within minutes, the clouds closed in again, and the sky returned to its previous darkness.

—*Yijian Zhi*, c. 1198

In March of 1356, two suns swung around each other.

—*Xu Zizhi Tongjian*, 1801

In March of 1356, during late afternoon, the sky suddenly became dim and yellow, as if shrouded in haze and fog. People in the marketplace were clamoring: "There are two suns in the sky!" Indeed, two suns were seen intersecting and then separating, and after separating, they merged again.

—*Lejiao Siyu*, c. 1363

In the autumn of 1602, a star in the shape of an egg appeared one night, its light scattering and illuminating the ground. It was followed by two smaller stars. And later, two other stars—one large and one small—continually flew loops around it.

—*Tongling County Chronicles of Anhui*, 1757

One night in July of 1908, a fiery star flew in midair, coming from the north and heading south. It was disc-shaped and was lit like an electric lamp. Suddenly, its light withdrew inward, and the object disappeared.

—*The Zaoqiang County Chronicles of Hebei*, 1931

CONTEMPORARY ASIAN REPORTS

May 1951 during the Korean War
Chorwon, South Korea
Primary Witnesses: Multiple U.S. military personnel including PFC Francis P. Wall and approximately 25 other soldiers

While preparing to bombard a village near Chorwon, PFC Francis P. Wall and his regiment observed a strange luminescent object resembling "a jack-o-lantern" moving across the hillside. The object descended toward a village where artillery fire was active, demonstrating extraordinary capabilities by passing directly through artillery airbursts without sustaining damage. Suddenly, the object changed color from a glowing orange to a pulsating blue-green light. Wall, after getting permission, fired armor-piercing bullets from an M-1 rifle at it. They made contact—a metallic "ding" on each impact—and the object began moving erratically, swaying side to side, lights flashing from it.

The soldiers then reported being "swept by some form of a ray" emitted in pulsating waves from the object, the ray visible only when aimed directly at them. Those affected experienced a burning, tingling sensation throughout their bodies that Wall described as a penetrating feeling. The unit took shelter in underground bunkers as the craft hovered above until it departed at a 45-degree angle. Three days later, the entire company was evacuated for medical attention. All affected soldiers were diagnosed with dysentery and exhibited abnormally elevated white blood cell counts. These symptoms were later noted by researcher Dr. Richard F. Haines as consistent with radiation exposure. Wall himself suffered significant long-term health effects, including permanent weight loss, chronic stomach problems, and episodes of disorientation and memory loss. This case was one of at least 42 separate UFO incidents reported by military personnel throughout the 37-month Korean conflict, creating one of the most substantial collections of UFO documentation from trained observers in a combat setting.

June 28, 1967
Taipei, Taiwan
Primary Witnesses: Tsai Chang-hung (brother of renowned astronomer Tsai Chang-hsien), numerous Taipei residents including student Liao Kuang-sung, and other callers to the Taipei Yuanshan Observatory

Tsai Chang-hung was visiting his brother—a renowned astronomer—at the Taipei Yuanshan Observatory on the evening of June 28, 1967, when a bright disc-shaped object emitting red-orange light appeared in the sky. It flew from northeast to southwest, hovered for about ten seconds near the Big Dipper, made a sharp 180-degree turn, and vanished. The whole thing lasted roughly two and a half minutes.

About 50 minutes later, the object reappeared. Tsai Chang-hung observed it through a 5-inch naval telescope, clearly seeing the UFO's exterior—a brilliant disc with an intense orange-red glow emanating from its entire outer shell, surpassing Venus in brightness. He quickly mounted his camera to the telescope's platform and captured three photographs. One image showed the UFO in its entirety and is considered the first authenticated UFO photograph in Taiwan's history.

That same night, numerous witnesses across Taipei contacted the Yuanshan Observatory reporting similar sightings. They described a cigar-shaped luminous object that repeatedly appeared and disappeared in the night sky. Among the witnesses was Liao Kuang-sung, a student from Taipei Municipal Jianguo High School, who had a close encounter near the Taipei District Court. He described a disc-shaped object so large it nearly spanned the width of the street and reported being terrified as the object silently passed overhead.

January 6, 1969, 1:52 AM, during the Vietnam War
Chu Lai, Vietnam
Primary Witnesses: Multiple U.S. military personnel including observation tower guards

As recorded in the daily journal of the 23rd Infantry Division's Chu Lai Defense Command, at 1:52 AM, Tower 72 personnel reported an unusual egg-shaped object roughly 15–20 feet across flying into their area about 700 meters in front of their position at azimuth 310°. The object glowed when it moved and approached slowly over the ammunition supply point before landing in the defense perimeter. Control tower radar detected nothing, and witnesses noted the object made no sound as it moved. This sighting is particularly credible since it was recorded in official military documentation by personnel whose mission was coordinating ground defense of the Chu Lai Defense Sector, located on the Vietnamese coast about 40 miles southeast of Da Nang. The base's defense system included numbered observation towers ringing the perimeter, which routinely reported anything unusual or potentially threatening to the base.

Summer 1972
Minowayama, Fukushima Prefecture, Japan
Primary Witnesses: Four climbers

While hiking up Minowayama mountain west of Senganmori, 25-year-old Kinoshita and three friends observed a helmet-shaped object hovering motionlessly in the sky for approximately 10–15 minutes, as if suspended in place. The object was a distinctive oxidized silver color comparable to a one-yen coin and was estimated to be around 30 centimeters long. The four witnesses were stunned into silence for about half a minute by the sight. The object completely vanished when the hikers attempted to reach the summit for a better view. This case represents one of many sightings reported within a 30–40-kilometer radius around Senganmori mountain, an area known for unusual magnetic properties.

August 9, 1974
Near an Indonesian island (108°13'E, 0°38'N)
Primary Witnesses: Third Officer Hsieh Chin-tsai and two crew members aboard the Taiwanese fishing vessel "Seal No. 1"

At 11:29 PM, the crew of the Taiwanese fishing vessel Seal No. 1 was sailing near the western coast of an Indonesian island, close to the equator, when a bright red object appeared in the sky. It was elliptical, softly glowing, with slightly reduced luminosity toward its center. Its size, more than ten times the diameter of the moon, shocked the witnesses. The object traveled at high speed from west to east at low altitude, vanishing over the horizon after approximately one minute. Upon reaching Jakarta, the crew sent a report to Tsai Chang-hsien, Director of the Yuan-shan Observatory, who classified it as a UFO sighting.

October 23, 1978, 8:40 PM
Gansu Province, China
Primary Witnesses: Air Force pilots and ground support personnel at an airfield near the Gobi Desert

Air Force personnel at an airfield near the Gobi Desert were watching an outdoor movie when a massive object suddenly appeared above them at an altitude of 6,000 to 8,000 meters. Spanning over 1,000 meters in length, it was had two brilliant lights, one at the front and one at the tail. It moved east to west, covering half the sky. The sighting lasted several minutes.

October 28, 1979
Taipei, Taiwan
Primary Witnesses: Over ten citizens from Yangmingshan, Nanshijiao, Nangang, Shuangxi, Songshan, and the Yuanshan Grand Hotel areas of Taipei

Multiple witnesses reported seeing a luminous object in Taipei. Ms. Hsu from Nanshijiao described it as an oval larger than the moon, radiating bright, sunset-colored light. Mr. Gao, a medical student, and his classmates observed the object split into three parts before disappearing within half an hour. Mr. Ma, a graduate student from the Central Police University, described a disk-shaped object with silver windows encircling its perimeter. From Yuanshan restaurant, Chen Yüeh-chuan and colleagues observed a similarly described object, noting red lights shining from the small windows. According to the Yuanshan Observatory's assessment, the object was below the cloud layer at an altitude of less than 1,500 meters, located approximately 6–7 kilometers west of Yuanshan above Xinzhuang District.

July 24, 1981, 10:30 PM
Multiple Provinces, China
Primary Witnesses: Over one million people, including astronomers, meteorologists, military personnel, and civilians across Tibet, Sichuan, Qinghai, Gansu, Shaanxi, Ningxia, Henan, Hubei, Anhui, and Jiangsu

More than a million people watched as a brilliant object glided across the night sky, slowly spinning and ejecting radiant material from its center so that the whole formation had the appearance of a massive, unfolding spiral. Witnesses described five or six distinct yellowish-white spiral rings, each edged with delicate halos of pale green and blue light, stretching high above the horizon. Some estimates that the pattern spanned nearly 100 kilometers across. The entire structure gave the impression of a massive, glowing vortex spinning in place high above the Earth, and visible over a 2,000-kilometer range across western China. It stayed that way for over two hours. The event was documented by astronomical observatories across the region and reported by Xinhua News. It remains one of the most extensively witnessed and well-documented UFO sightings in Chinese history.

April 4, 1984
Taichung City, Taiwan
Primary Witnesses: Mu Tzu-wei, President of the National Chung Hsing University Astronomy Society, and three classmates

Mu Tzu-wei was conducting astronomical observations with three classmates when they spotted a moon-sized green glowing object. It was moving slowly westward at first—then suddenly shot southward at more than twice its original speed, zigzagged, and resumed its westward course.

November 17, 1986, 5:11 PM
Alaska Airspace
Primary Witnesses: Captain Kenju Terauchi, Co-pilot Takanori Tamefuji, Flight Engineer Yoshio Tsukuba

The Japanese crew of a Japan Airlines Boeing 747 cargo freighter encountered three unidentified objects while flying over Alaska. Captain Kenju Terauchi, a veteran pilot with over 10,000 flight hours, along with his co-pilot and flight engineer, first noticed two objects at 5:11 PM while flying at 35,000 feet. Through the cockpit window, he could see rectangular arrays of rapidly blinking orange, green, white, and amber lights—like strings of bulbs arranged in geometric patterns. He initially assumed they were some kind of military aircraft because of their size. The craft positioned themselves about 2,000 feet to the far left and slightly below the 747, maintaining this formation as the jet continued on its course.

At about 5:19 PM, the two craft abruptly slid across the sky and braked into position directly in front of the cockpit, only 500 to 1,000 feet ahead, stacked one above the other. In making this maneuver, they displayed what Terauchi described as a complete disregard for inertia and gravity and appeared to fire some kind of "reverse thrust," flaring into dazzling brilliance for several seconds. The light was so intense that Terauchi could feel warmth on his face through the cockpit window. The craft accompanied the 747 for several minutes, matching every course adjustment.

Air traffic control was notified at this point but could not detect any traffic in the indicated position.

At around 5:23 PM, the two small craft suddenly broke away and dropped toward the eastern horizon, disappearing within seconds. In their place, a pale band of light appeared on the left front side of the jet. It resolved into the outline of a gigantic, walnut-shaped craft. Terauchi estimated it to be roughly "two times bigger than an aircraft carrier," about a thousand feet long.

The massive object paced the 747 despite the jet's attempts to outmaneuver it via several turns and attempts at descent. It occasionally disappeared from view only to reappear moments later in a different position. Unlike the first two craft, several Anchorage air traffic controllers confirmed the radar signature of this object, although it appeared and disappeared from their screens multiple times. When Anchorage Center offered to scramble military aircraft, Captain Terauchi declined, fearing for everyone's safety. Meanwhile, military radar at Elmendorf Regional Operations Control Center also tracked the object. Finally, as JAL1628 approached Fairbanks, the mysterious craft suddenly disappeared.

The Federal Aviation Administration conducted an extensive investigation, interviewing all crew members and reviewing radar data. FAA Division Chief John Callahan later testified that during a subsequent meeting attended by representatives of the FBI, CIA, and President Reagan's Scientific Study Team, all present were told that the incident never happened. They were instructed to surrender all documentation, though he secretly retained copies. Despite attempts at suppression, the case generated international attention after the FAA's early confirmation to reporters helped propel it into the media, making it one of the most thoroughly documented aviation UAP encounters in history.

August 27, 1987, 7:35 PM
Shanghai and Eastern China
Primary Witnesses: Air Force pilot Mao Xuecheng, Shanghai Meteorological Bureau official Chen Feng, Shanghai Guanghua Middle School teacher Zhang Zhengyong, Air Force flight controller Ping Xiaojun (Hangzhou), three aerospace engineers at Wuxi's 738 Sanatorium, and military personnel and residents on Shengsi Island, Zhejiang Province

Multiple witnesses across eastern China reported an extraordinary unidentified flying object that exhibited spiral rotation and electromagnetic effects. Chen Feng at Shanghai's Xujiahui meteorological station first observed what he described as "a circular object in the southwestern sky that continuously rotated in a spiral pattern, with an orange-red tail behind it," and that grew from a bright point to plate size before disappearing.

Teacher Zhang Zhengyong described the phenomenon as orange-yellow in color, with an intensely bright core surrounded by a spiral made up of three concentric rings of light. The entire structure rotated clockwise, completing one full rotation approximately every two seconds.

Air Force pilot Mao Xuecheng encountered the same phenomenon while returning from patrol and pursued the object for two minutes and 45 seconds over Jiading County. He described it as resembling "a straw hat shape, trailing a very long tail behind it, somewhat similar to a rocket launch," and measured it moving at several times his aircraft's speed.

Simultaneous sightings were also reported by flight controller Ping Xiaojun in Hangzhou and three aerospace engineers in Wuxi, who observed a "plate-sized object" with an estimated 300–400-centimeter diameter flying in spiral trajectories. The incident produced widespread electromagnetic effects.

When the object passed over Shengsi Island in Zhejiang province, the power plant suddenly lost electricity despite normal operations, watches stopped functioning, and the island was plunged into darkness while the object itself illuminated the area so that it was "as bright as daylight." The event received extensive coverage in major Chinese media, including reports in *People's Daily* and *Zhejiang Daily*, making it one of the most well-documented UFO cases in Chinese history.

March 18, 1991, 6:12 PM
Shanghai Hongqiao Airport, China
Primary Witnesses: Pilot Zhu Zhaoyuan and the flight crew of Flight 3556 from Shanghai to Jinan, air traffic controllers at Shanghai Hongqiao Airport including ground controller Jin Xin, and residents in the Wusong, Xinzhuang, and Bund areas

Flight 3556 from Shanghai to Jinan encountered an unidentified flying object shortly after takeoff. Between 6:12 PM and 6:26 PM, the crew observed what initially appeared as a single fireball transform into a formation of multiple fireballs whose glow turned black, before they consolidated into two distinct objects —one round and one rectangular. They maneuvered around the aircraft, alternately moving closer and backing off, forcing pilot Zhu Zhaoyuan to change course multiple times to avoid collision. The incident ended when the objects suddenly merged back into one, shot straight up, and disappeared. According to *Xinmin Evening News*, reporter Cui Yilin received calls from residents in the Wusong, Xinzhuang, and Bund areas who also reported sightings of the object.

The encounter resulted in over 10 minutes of recorded communication between Zhu and ground controller Jin Xin that narrated the unfolding incident. This recording remained undisclosed for 17 years until it was revealed at the "Major UFO Incidents Academic Conference" in Shanghai in June 2008.

December 16, 1994, 4:30 PM
Taipei, Taiwan
Primary Witnesses: Multiple residents across Taipei, including Ms. Sun Hui-chuan, Mr. Lin Shih-jen, and Mr. Chiu Shui-wen

Five disc-shaped objects appeared near the Presidential Office at 4:30 PM—one large luminous craft accompanied by four smaller ones. While the large luminous craft matched the classic flying saucer shape from UFO literature, the others were oval with a black metallic color. All moved slowly and steadily across the sky.

Mr. Chiu Shui-wen, a 42-year-old plumber, chased the objects by motorcycle as they traveled toward Hebin Park. He tried to photograph them, but they were too far away for clear shots. The whole sighting lasted about five minutes.

In total, at least 25 people from different locations across Taipei reported the same phenomenon to various news agencies that day.

January 5, 1996, 6:10 PM
Suhua Highway, Taiwan
Primary Witnesses: Approximately 40–50 people, including drivers and passengers

At 6:10 PM, roughly 40 to 50 witnesses watched a huge gray disc-shaped object hovering over the Pacific Ocean along Taiwan's coastal Suhua Highway. The craft, consistently described as big as a 40,000-ton cargo ship, maintained a distance of 50 to 100 meters above the water. Witnesses reported that the object featured eight extremely bright lights arranged in a distinct Z-pattern. During the encounter, seven of these lights suddenly shut off simultaneously, leaving only the uppermost light illuminated. This was followed by a low-frequency rumbling sound that lasted 45 to 60 seconds. In the final moments, the remaining light swept in a circle like it was scanning, while the craft vibrated slightly before shooting straight up and disappearing from sight in less than a second. The entire sighting lasted about 10 minutes.

March 10, 1996, 5:06 PM
Taoyuan, Taiwan
Primary Witnesses: Captain Kung Chia-chi and Co-pilot Lu Ben-hsien of China Airlines Flight 017

China Airlines Flight 017, carrying 294 passengers from Hawaii via Tokyo, encountered an unidentified flying object while preparing to land at Taoyuan Chiang Kai-shek Airport. At 5:06 PM, as the aircraft was in airspace 9 nautical miles offshore following Taipei Approach Control's instructions to descend from 3,000 to 2,000 feet, Captain Kung Chia-chi suddenly heard warning signals from the collision avoidance radar. He spotted an unidentified flying object on the radar screen, two to five nautical miles to the left of Flight 017, between the aircraft and the airport.

Co-pilot Lu Ben-hsien contacted air traffic control to verify the flying object, but controllers reported their radar showed no such aircraft. They noted there were naval vessels in the area and suggested it might be radar signals from ships. As Flight 017 continued descending through clouds, the radar warned that the UFO was directly ahead, presenting an immediate collision risk. Kung immediately executed emergency evasive maneuvers to the left, and the object moved to the right side and then the rear of the aircraft.

Despite the air traffic controllers' suggested explanation, both pilots insisted that what they saw did not resemble the radar signatures of military ships. The encounter lasted about five minutes before the flight safely landed at Chiang Kai-shek Airport at 5:18 PM. Most passengers and cabin crew reported experiencing unusual turbulence during descent, though they were unaware of the UFO encounter.

1997–2000s
Khao Kala Hill, Nakhon Sawan Province, Thailand
Primary Witnesses: Jaroen Raepeth, Wassana Chuensamnaun, and multiple residents and meditation group members

In 1997, retired military officer Sergeant-Major Cherd Chuensamnaun told his family that he had begun receiving telepathic messages from extraterrestrial beings during deep meditation. His daughter Wassana, a professional nurse at the time, initially rejected the claim and challenged him to provide proof.

The following day, according to the family's later testimony, something happened inside their house that none of them could explain. Jaroen Raepeth, Wassana's brother-in-law, and another family member were suddenly lifted from their seats and rotated in place, eventually moving out of the house and into the yard as though pulled by an invisible force. Jaroen described the experience afterward as being fully conscious but completely unable to control his body. He noted there was no dizziness, pain, or fear —only complete loss of motor control for several minutes.

In the years that followed, the area around Khao Kala gained a reputation as a hotspot for UFO sightings and anomalous encounters. Wassana eventually resigned from nursing and committed herself to facilitating what she described as a human-alien contact group rooted in meditation. Members began reporting repeated sightings of presumed non-human entities in nearby agricultural fields. These beings were generally described as thin, humanlike figures with metallic, reflective skin, seen emerging from spherical or disc-shaped craft before fading from sight—dematerializing, as several witnesses put it.

April 30, 1998
Bandarawela, Sri Lanka
Primary Witnesses: Multiple individuals including school children, doctors, and local residents

On Thursday, April 30, 1998, a UFO incident designated as case BAN-CE-II by the Sri Lanka UFO Research Association (SLUFORA) occurred at Adikaram Primary School in Bandarawela. Eight-year-old Indika Sampath Dissanayake arrived at school around 6:30 AM and, after hearing a sharp noise, witnessed a large disc-shaped object with legs on the playground that blazed with bright red and yellow lights before taking off at high speed. Ten-year-old Harsha Ellawalagedera, described by teachers as a promising candidate for scholarship exams, backed up the sighting. The object was roughly eight feet across and seven feet tall and made a soft purring noise as it flew off. Harsha's friend, Priyanjith, also observed the object as it flew up and away. The children also reported similar objects had been seen hovering above the school previously. They nicknamed them "koka" (stork).

Striking phenomena were not limited to Adikaram school that day, as multiple witnesses throughout Bandarawela reported similar sightings. Around 7:45 PM near St. Joseph's grounds, sixteen-year-old Sheran de Silva from St. Thomas' College encountered a disc-shaped flying object that beamed down a large column of bright red-yellow light which engulfed his body before he fled in fear. Dr. P. Ramachandran of the Bandarawela District Hospital and his wife observed an unusual "laser-like" red-yellow beam of light shining down from the sky that same evening while driving home. During the investigation it was disclosed that his colleague Dr. Kamani Pushpa Kumara of Diyatalawa hospital had witnessed a disc-shaped object flashing red, yellow, and green lights while stargazing with her children in mid-March, noting it was distinctly different from military aircraft from the nearby Diyatalawa camp.

October 3, 1998, 11:50 AM
Kunming, Yunnan Province, China
Primary Witnesses: Han Jianwei and family members visiting a family tomb site on the back mountain of Qiongzhu Temple in the northwestern suburbs of Kunming

While picnicking after visiting his father-in-law's tomb, Han Jianwei and four other family members spotted a highly luminous silver-white object hovering several hundred meters above a high-rise building approximately 10 kilometers away over downtown Kunming. The object disappeared then reappeared about three minutes later to the right of its original position. At this time, Han grabbed his family's video camera and began filming.

Through the camera's zoom lens, Han observed the object dramatically transform. It first appeared as an intensely bright golden sphere wrapped by what Han described as "two pieces of black rubber" at the top and bottom. After approximately 30 seconds of continuous filming, the object flashed and changed into what Han described as "a large diamond shaped by four smaller flying diamonds."

The four smaller diamonds subsequently transformed into nine glowing points still arranged in a diamond pattern, each radiating golden light. The four cardinal points—top, bottom, left, and right—blazed with particular intensity, while the corner and central lights appeared somewhat dimmer.

Despite his hands shaking throughout the whole encounter, Han managed to capture over two minutes of video footage before the object gradually dimmed and vanished. This was approximately 15 minutes after the initial sighting. The family waited another hour, but the object did not reappear.

The video was later examined by Zhang Yifang, Physics Professor at Yunnan University and Director of the Kunming

UFO Research Association, who confirmed its authenticity and ruled out conventional explanations such as atmospheric electrical discharge, weather balloons, insects, and known aircraft. On November 22, 1999, the footage was publicly premiered at the Chinese Aerospace Science Exhibition, where it drew considerable attention as China's first video documentation of a UFO encounter.

October 19, 1998, 11:00 PM
Cangzhou, Hebei Province, China
Primary Witnesses: Air Force personnel, radar operators, and approximately 160 civilians

The incident began when Air Force radar sounded an alarm, followed quickly by three additional radar confirmations of an unknown entity moving directly above the airport and rapidly traveling northeast. Ground crew simultaneously spotted a bright point of light overhead that initially resembled a star but soon transformed into two side-by-side lights—one red, one white—that rotated continuously before merging back into a single object.

As the object dropped lower, witnesses described it as also growing larger and taking the shape of a "short-stemmed mushroom" with multiple lights on its underside, including one larger light that continuously beamed toward the ground.

At 11:30 PM, radar operators confirmed the object had moved to hover above Qing County at precisely 1,500 meters altitude. Air traffic control verified no civilian aircraft were in the vicinity, and military night training had ended thirty minutes earlier. Commanders placed the base on first-class combat readiness.

Deputy Commander Liu Ming and Squadron Leader Hu Shaoheng scrambled in J-6 jet fighters to the object's coordinates. They quickly identified it: circular with an arched top and flat bottom, rows of lights underneath, a downward-pointing beam, and a red light on its edge—resembling a "straw hat" or "teacup lid." Following orders to approach, they pushed their throttle toward the object, but when they were around 4,000 meters away, it suddenly surged upward. The pilots climbed to 3,000 meters, but the object, with superior speed, positioned itself directly above their aircraft.

The pilots tried several strategic maneuvers, first dropping altitude and changing direction to create distance, then suddenly accelerating and performing a loop maneuver to gain altitude advantage, but the object simply repositioned itself to remain above them. Deputy Commander Liu released the trigger safety and positioned his targeting reticle on the object, requesting permission to engage, but Commander Li Suolin ordered them to identify what it was first.

Despite maximum throttle, they still could not close the distance, and when they reached 12,000 meters, the object climbed to 20,000 meters. Finally, with their fuel warnings flashing red, the aircraft were ordered back to base while ground radar continued tracking. By the time two more advanced fighter jets prepared for takeoff, the object had vanished from radar. Approximately 160 civilians on the ground witnessed the entire event.

June 30, 2002, 10:10 PM
Multiple Provinces across China
Primary Witnesses: Military pilots, air force personnel, astronomy enthusiasts, and thousands of civilians across at least eight provinces including Jiangsu, Henan, Shaanxi, Sichuan, Gansu, Anhui, Ningxia, and Hebei

At roughly 10:10 PM at Dazu Air Base in Sichuan Province, a military pilot returning to base at about 600 meters altitude encountered an unidentified object with bright yellow lights flying parallel to his aircraft at the same altitude, roughly 400 meters to his right. When the pilot turned to fly back, the object immediately repositioned itself to his left side, maintaining the same parallel course. Concerned about a potential collision, the pilot immediately landed.

By 10:20 PM, similar sightings were being reported across northwestern China. An unknown object blasting intense, fan-shaped light was visible simultaneously from provinces including Ningxia, Jiangsu, Anhui, Henan, Sichuan, Shaanxi, and Gansu. Witnesses in northern Jiangsu described an object like a rising sun, shooting fan-shaped light similar to a spotlight with light rays undulating like waves. The phenomenon's simultaneity across such vast distances meant the object was flying at exceptionally high altitude.

At approximately 10:25 PM, Chen Shiwen, who was attending a funeral 30 kilometers from Lanzhou in Gansu Province, observed and filmed an object flying slowly from due east to west with a bright tail. After about two minutes, the object halted mid-air; its bright tail disappeared, and then the object dimmed and vanished. About a minute later, it reappeared with even greater brightness, this time spiraling upward toward the south. After rotating for about ten seconds, the object transformed into what Chen described as a "sycee shape"—the form of an ancient ingot, like a small, shallow boat with upturned sides—before gradually disappearing. His video documentation of the five-minute event became important evidence of the sighting.

Around the same time, military personnel at Dazu Air Base observed a cone-shaped pillar of light in the sky, illuminating the ground like a powerful searchlight before slowly fading away like a patch of white clouds over the next eight minutes.

The widespread nature of this sighting across multiple provinces, the consistent descriptions from military and civilian witnesses, and the photographic evidence make this one of China's most significant mass UFO sightings.

August 28, 2002, 9:07 PM
Multiple Provinces, China
Primary Witnesses: Hundreds of observers across multiple provinces including firefighters at Huian Chemical Factory in Hu County

On Aug 28, 2002, a local newspaper received over a hundred calls from readers in Dingbian, Yongshou, Sanyuan, Lintong, Lantian, Hu County of Xi'an, and other locations, all reporting the same phenomenon.

Firefighters at Huian Chemical Factory provided a detailed account. At 9:07 PM, while chatting outside their station, firefighter Wang Jun noticed a bright spot moving in the northeastern sky. According to his colleague Zhang Lin, it was "coin-shaped, radiating a pale white light similar to moonlight but with warmer tones than the cold light of stars."

The object, which had a small cylindrical section beneath its circular form, moved from northeast to southwest, then westward, gradually expanding "like fog" until it appeared "about three times the size of the moon." It faded away around 9:14 PM. Similar reports came from Liangshan, Xuzhou, Zaoqiang, Chengdu, Lanzhou, as well as Inner Mongolia and Henan province, with witnesses all noting the timing around 9:10 PM. A teacher from Liangshan pinpointed the object's position near the handle of the Big Dipper constellation.

July 7, 2010, 8:26 PM
Hangzhou, China
Primary Witnesses: Flight crew of commercial airliners, air traffic controllers, and Hangzhou residents including Ma Shijun

On the evening of July 7, 2010, Hangzhou's Xiaoshan International Airport was thrown into chaos due to a highly unusual aerial sighting. At around 8:40 PM, a commercial airliner crew preparing for landing spotted a twinkling orb in the sky and quickly informed air traffic control. A second flight crew corroborated the sighting during the same window. Despite the object not showing up on radar, authorities acted immediately, shutting down the airport from 8:45 PM to 9:41 PM. In total, 18 flights were either delayed or diverted, affecting roughly 2,000 passengers.

At 8:26 PM, local resident Ma Shijun was taking a nighttime walk with his wife when he suddenly felt a beam of light pass over his head. Looking up, he saw a "streak of bright, white light flying across the sky," noticeably faster and larger than any commercial airplane.

Ma did not hear any sound from the object, which appeared to expand as it approached. The sighting lasted less than 30 seconds before the object "retreated rapidly into the distance." Ma reacted quickly enough to capture five photographs. These become central to the subsequent investigation and widely circulated in Chinese media.

Dozens of other Hangzhou residents offered similar accounts, describing a cigar-shaped or elongated object, illuminated by red and white light, flying at a relatively low altitude. Some photos these residents took showed a comet-like object with a tail bathed in golden light. Despite clear eyewitness testimony and photographic evidence, the identity of the object remains controversial. Theories range from military tests (including the possibility of a secret Chinese missile or aircraft), to "light reflecting off a plane," and outright speculation about extraterrestrial craft.

Officially, authorities attributed the shutdown of Xiaoshan International Airport to a private aircraft, but this explanation was met with swift and widespread skepticism due to the unlikelihood of a private aircraft causing disruption on such a scale at a major airport.

It's worth noting that on September 11, 2024, a similar shutdown took place at Tianjin Binhai International Airport. This time officials cited drone activity as the cause. However, detailed eyewitness accounts, including photos and video, generated widespread doubt. The incident fueled online debate about whether Chinese airports were again experiencing the same kind of unexplained phenomena seen in Hangzhou in 2010.

March 11-12, 2011
Fukushima Prefecture, Japan
Primary Witnesses: Multiple witnesses including Chief Monk Tomonori Izumi and local residents

In the aftermath of the devastating Fukushima Daiichi nuclear disaster that began on March 11, 2011, numerous witnesses throughout the affected region reported an extraordinary surge in anomalous aerial phenomena, from strange lights to strange shapes. Chief Monk Tomonori Izumi of the Enmyoin Temple observed multiple unidentified flying objects in the skies above the disaster zone during the period when radioactive material was actively leaking from the damaged reactors, and multiple independent witnesses corroborated these sightings.

August 2012–October 2012
Ladakh Region, India
Primary Witnesses: Multiple Indian Army and Indo-Tibetan Border Police Force (ITBP) personnel

Between August 1 and October 15, 2012, an ITBP unit stationed in Thakung near Pangong Tso Lake reported over 100 sightings of mysterious luminous objects along the India-China border. These glowing yellowish orbs were repeatedly seen rising from the Chinese horizon, then moving across the sky at a measured pace for three to five hours before disappearing. The consistency and frequency of these sightings prompted the Army's 14 Corps, responsible for military deployment in the Kargil-Leh region, to send formal reports to Army Headquarters in Delhi and eventually to the Prime Minister's Office. What particularly troubled officials was the objects' appearance during both the day and the night, showing movement patterns inconsistent with known aircraft.

In September 2012, responding to the persistent sightings, the Army deployed sophisticated equipment including a mobile ground-based radar unit and a spectrum analyzer to a mountaintop near Pangong Lake to investigate. Despite extensive analysis by multiple intelligence and research agencies, including the National Technical Research Organisation (NTRO) and Defence Research and Development Organisation (DRDO), the objects remained unidentified. Military officials confirmed these were not Chinese drones or satellites, as those are tracked and logged separately.

PART II
DISCUSSION

The Universe is not obliged to conform to what we consider comfortable or plausible.

—Carl Sagan, *Pale Blue Dot*

ANCIENT ACCOUNTS
AND MODERN PARALLELS

Some people crave only the new. But we dig old stuff too: bones, sketches, teeth, ancient erotic paraphernalia, and, perhaps most of all, old scrolls that reveal our ancestors were not so different from us.

The earliest known brain surgery, for example, dates back 7,000 years, with Neolithic trepanation techniques so sophisticated they remain recognizable in modern neurosurgery. Ancient Egyptians devised pregnancy tests using barley and wheat seeds that responded to hormonal changes. If the seeds sprouted, new life was (quite poetically) confirmed.

Prefiguring the burgeoning worker, murder, and sex bot industry today, the classical text *Liezi* describes how, around 1000 BCE, engineer Yan Shi presented King Mu with a life-sized automaton. The machine walked with such natural strides that observers mistook it for human. When its chin was touched, it would sing in perfect pitch and perform lifelike gestures, including winking flirtatiously. The king was so unnerved that he reportedly threatened to execute Yan Shi on the spot.

And then there's Democritus who gave us atomic theory in

5th century BCE, Anaximander who proposed humans evolved from fish-like creatures in 6th century BCE, and philosopher Shao Yong who developed a binary mathematical system for divination using the *I Ching* in the 11th century. Six hundred years later, German mathematician Gottfried Leibniz credited Shao Yong's work when developing binary arithmetic, the foundation of modern computer code that sees reality as patterns of 0's and 1's rather than yin and yang. Add to these the Baghdad Battery: a 2,000-year-old clay jar that generates electric current when filled with acidic liquid, predating Alessandro Volta's invention of the battery by over 1,500 years.

Of course, such legitimate precedents appear alongside misidentifications that reach too far. The "Dorchester Pot," a metal vessel allegedly recovered from million-year-old rock in 1852 and heralded as evidence of an advanced prehistoric civilization, was later thought by some investigators to simply be a Victorian-era candlestick holder that fell into excavation debris.

Ancient astronaut theories are another dramatic example of what can go right and wrong with speculative historical analysis. We shouldn't assume that every feat of ancient engineering required patient alien instruction or represents remnants of a lost advanced civilization, but we shouldn't dismiss all historical accounts of strange flying objects as clouds or comets either, nor deny similarities between today's encounters with UFOs and yesterday's with divine non-human entities from the sky.

After all, the astronomer Carl Sagan himself, despite famously insisting that "extraordinary claims require extraordinary evidence," originated the ancient astronaut hypothesis in his 1966 *Intelligent Life in the Universe*. [1]

However, this proposal was in the spirit of sharing a speculative possibility rather than making a hard claim. So it was that in 1979's *Broca's Brain*, Sagan criticized books like Erich von Däniken's *Chariots of the Gods* as too uncritical, going so far as to apologize for inspiring other "ancient astronaut" publications. [2]

While some argue Sagan lumped all later ancient astronaut theorists together, he nevertheless pointed toward the proper spirit of comparative work. It should be undertaken not with pre-assumed certainty but with open-minded curiosity—an attitude he himself articulated in *Broca's Brain*, declaring: "It is the tension between creativity and skepticism that has produced the stunning and unexpected findings of science."

It's this spirit that guides *Stars That Pause*. We examine parallels between ancient and modern UAP (unidentified anomalous phenomena) accounts and explore competing interpretations without insisting on a definitive explanation. [3]

Could UAPs be intelligent plasma formations, as Italian astrophysicist Massimo Teodorani proposes? Or are they insensate plasma that uncannily mimic intentionality, the hypothesis offered by researcher Zou Yousuo when discussing a 1988 basketball-sized UFO that paced a Chinese commercial airliner?

Are we witnessing visitors from parallel dimensions, distant galaxies, or our own future timelines? Or are we encountering, as Carl Jung suggested, manifestations of humanity's shared unconscious—"psychoid" events revealing reality as fundamentally malleable and operating like a vast consensually shared lucid dream? [4] Alternatively, might these phenomena be evidence of an ancient species that abandoned (or never possessed) physical bodies and lives uploaded in a vast quantum cloud? [5] [6]

Our interest in this topic originated during our work on *The Shadow Book of Ji Yun*, a collection of strange accounts compiled by Ji Yun, a nationally acclaimed 18th-century Chinese scholar who also served as head of the Ministry of War and China's Imperial Librarian. [7]

We were particularly intrigued by his autobiographical

"Guests from the Sky," an early Chinese UFO abduction narrative, and stunned that one of China's foremost intellectuals and military leaders had documented a UFO abduction centuries before the 1961 case of Betty and Barney Hill—and in a completely different cultural context at that.

That discovery sent us deeper into China's extensive historical archives in search of other UFO reports. We found hundreds, thanks to China's tradition of meticulous record keeping. From these, we set aside cases explainable by conventional phenomena and concentrated on accounts that exhibited the "Five Observables," the criteria that Luis Elizondo developed while directing the Pentagon's Advanced Aerospace Threat Identification Program from 2010 to 2017.

Elizondo's framework distinguishes truly anomalous objects from the usual suspects—such as drones or advanced aircraft—or the unusual, such as rare atmospheric events or Cousin Ronnie's lawn chair hot-rodded with balloons. His criteria include anti-gravity lift, instantaneous acceleration, hypersonic velocity without sonic booms, trans-medium travel (seamlessly moving between air, water, and space), and low observability (appearing and vanishing suddenly, evading radar detection). To these, we also added elements particularly relevant to historical cases: such as coordinated formations of lights moving in synchronized patterns, and unnaturally bright lights (pulsing, scanning, or emitting directed beams) attached to larger objects.

When we apply these observables to our historical accounts, striking patterns emerge. [8]

Take the first piece in our "Sightings" section: the 1899 **"Ships Like Shells."** In it, we have a powerful example of why "UAP" has recently replaced UFO as the preferred terminology, as two UAPs hide in water before taking to the air [trans-medium travel and positive lift]. Like their modern counterparts, they demonstrate instantaneous acceleration and hypersonic velocity and are embedded with lights so powerful that they light up a daytime sky [attached unnatural lights].

The objects also trigger sudden violent weather, something else consistently observed across centuries of UAP encounters and other paranormal events, from poltergeist manifestations to temporal anomalies. [9]

Finally, there's the eerie soundlessness of the ship-like shells, remarkable enough for witnesses to comment upon it. This silence aligns with Elizondo's observation that UAPs often lack expected sound signatures—no sonic booms, no engine noise. It also echoes what folklorist Jenny Randles dubbed "The Oz Factor"—an abrupt dead silence as if nature just hit a mute button just before things get weird. Randles coined the term after noticing how often witnesses described this uncanny hush before paranormal encounters.

The far earlier and quite poignant 1166 C.E. **"Waiting for an Encounter"** gives us another object, this one orb-shaped, and also capable of trans-medium travel and positive lift. Here, the eyewitnesses are named, and connections are made to even earlier historical reports of similar objects, one immortalized by the Chinese poet Cui Boyi.

The orb remains the most reported UAP shape today. In August 2024, for example, NASA astronaut turned engineering consultant Leroy Chiao crossed paths with "two metallic spherical orbs," each approximately three feet in diameter, as he flew at 9,000 feet. The orbs zipped past just twenty feet off his wing, one above the other, and neither registered on his onboard electronic traffic display nor air-traffic control's radar.

In ancient Chinese accounts, this orb shape, along with unusual luminescence, led witnesses to refer to UAPs as otherworldly "pearls." But unlike its humble namesake, the pearl in "Waiting for an Encounter" is distinctly technological—anachronistically so. And its seamless surface, nested spherical chambers, and laser-like beam capable of focused flood-level intensity echo the unnaturally powerful light also portrayed in "Ships like Shells."

The story's most compelling element, however, is its moving conclusion: visitors traveling to the lake to sleep on boats night after night, ardently waiting for their own encounter. Their deep longing for the extraordinary prefigures modern UAP enthusiasts—from those practicing CE5 meditation to summon orbs in the California desert to those making pilgrimages to Roswell, New Mexico; Nevada's Extraterrestrial Highway; or Thailand's Khao Kala, where mysterious aerial phenomena have long been reported.

"Stars That Pause," excerpted from the 10th century *Tang Dynasty Astronomy Chronicles*, fascinates for several reasons: from the object's ability to both move and hover in the air [positive lift] to the dazzling yellowish-red light glowing from its upper portion [attached unnatural lights].

Most notable is its zigzagging movement, also seen in contemporary UAPs, such as those observed over India's Kudankulam Nuclear Power Plant in 2024, and also recorded on video by Indian Police Service investigator Syed Abdul Kader. [10]

In our times, these zigzagging mysteries are sometimes explained away as satellites—a much harder claim to make in the tenth century when possession of a digital wristwatch would mark you as a great and fearsome wizard. But perhaps most remarkable is the field of smaller lights surrounding this bigger object. They move with it in a uniform manner [moving light fields] before suddenly vanishing.

Contemporary cases show similar coordinated light formations, as both separate from a main object's body or sometimes as part of it. The 1997 Arizona Phoenix Lights saw parallel lights advance across the sky in a synchronized pattern, with witnesses describing them as a huge carpenter's square composed of distinct luminous points. The Belgian UFO Wave of the late 1980s featured large, triangular UFOs with especially bright lighting at each corner, observed moving in unison and sometimes changing direction abruptly. Exhibiting multiple observables from instant acceleration to a lack of sound signatures like sonic booms, as well as generating lethal G-forces, these objects were tracked on military radar, pursued by Belgian Air Force F-16 fighters, and witnessed by thousands of civilians on the ground.

There are several classical Chinese records of wheel-like UFOs, a shape that appears in modern times as well. We've included three representative examples. Two of these, "**The Bird with Wheel-Like Wings I**" and "**The Bird with Wheel-Like Wings II**," are quite short. Recorded in 1573 in Jiaxing, and in 1575 in Pinghu, respectively, these accounts feature flying objects described as big as sailing ships and roughly "bird-shaped" with wheel-like wings. The earlier 1573 case, however, contains a detail absent from the 1575 case. Its witnesses note that the observed object, when it "raises its head" and "turns its tail" during flight, causes storms to erupt, bringing us back to our earlier observation about the connection between UAPs and sudden weather anomalies.

Just as we do today, ancient witnesses reached for familiar metaphors when confronted with the unfamiliar. The sea and sky provided their vocabulary: pearls, shells, birds, sailing ships —to try to tame with names that which defied easy categorization.

Not so though with "**The Wheel**," where we encounter an object so alien that no comparison is even attempted: an armored black wheel covered with lights. Its idiosyncratic strangeness brings to mind *Ezekiel* 10:10 where "angels" appear as "wheels within wheels," with rims "full of eyes." Ezekiel's account has often been cited for its techno-mechanical impression. "The Wheel" shares this. And once again, we find the phenomena linked to dramatic weather—"Whenever these objects appeared, the weather would turn stormy." While the subsequent damage to the town might be attributed to a tornado, the specific observation of the wheel by ten separate families suggests something stranger at work.

Attention to such details matters when generating hypotheses for UAP accounts and deciding which fit best. Is a light in the sky static or does it move slowly, counter to gravity? Is a dark shape a tornado or something struggling against its pull? Does a storm expose a "cloaked" UAP or does a UAP somehow cause the storm?

A great example of such critical attention appears in the autobiographical "**Red Flame in Flight**," its narrative inscribed directly on the painting depicting the event, a common Chinese practice. [11] This multimedia account documents an egg-shaped UAP with a strange glow over Nanjing's Zhuque Bridge on September 28, 1892, which was witnessed by the artist Wu Youru alongside a large crowd.

According to Wu, the object suddenly leapt "a great distance" into view [positive lift and instantaneous acceleration]. Then, as it slowly flew overhead, an excited crowd debated its identity, methodically working through and dismissing conventional explanations.

The impromptu investigators concluded the object moved too slowly and deliberately for an odd meteor and wasn't a peculiar paper lantern either (the weather balloon explanation of its era), owing to its appearance and its movement counter to the wind. [12]

Ovals are another common UFO shape. Renowned artist and theater set designer Nicholas Roerich details such an encounter in his 1929 travel diary *Altai-Himalaya*. On August 5, 1927, while an expedition party, including his family, camped by China's Qinghai Lake, they witnessed an oval craft.

Roerich writes: "On August fifth—something remarkable! We were in our camp in the Kukunor district not far from the Humboldt Chain. In the morning about half-past nine some of our caravaneers noticed a remarkably big black eagle flying above us. Seven of us began to watch this unusual bird. At this same moment another of our caravaneers remarked, 'There is something far above the bird.' And he shouted in his astonishment. We all saw, in a direction from north to south, something big and shiny reflecting the sun, like a huge oval moving at great speed. Crossing our camp this thing changed in its direction from south to southwest. And we saw how it disappeared in the intense blue sky. We even had time to take out field glasses and saw quite distinctly an oval form with shiny surface, one side of which was brilliant from the sun."

A similar Western case occurred on October 26, 1958, when Alvin Cohen and Phillip Small encountered an iridescent egg-shaped object while driving past Loch Raven Reservoir in Maryland. As they approached the object, their car suddenly died. Cowering yet spellbound, they watched the object hover until—following a flash of light and intense heat—the object rocketed upward and vanished. Afterward, Small and Cohen reported their faces felt badly sunburnt.

This incident caught the attention of the Air Force's *Project Blue Book* UAP investigation. After interviewing witnesses, including a 16-year-old boy and two lakefront restaurant employees who saw the same glowing object, investigator Lieutenant Bert R. Staples concluded, as reported in *The Baltimore Sun*: "It can be assumed that the sighting did actually occur [although] it remains unidentified."

And here is one last case that we could not resist referring to since it came on our radar as we were finishing this manuscript.

In late 2024/early 2025, Air Force veteran Jake Barber publicly emerged as a whistleblower with an extraordinary claim: he had retrieved non-human craft for classified programs, including a white, egg-shaped object. Three other veterans independently corroborated his account. [13]

The 1561 "**The Top**" from *The Zhenhai County Chronicle* offers something different, and perhaps even more bizarre: an object that transforms while flying. With a pointy top and broad base, the object descends slowly while lights pulse violently from its surface. There is no sound but rather the eerie Oz silence again. Suddenly, it swells ten times larger. Not approaching closer and thus seeming to expand. But a sudden and inexplicable shift in size. This "Wonderland" effect, the ability to radically alter size and shape, recurs throughout contemporary accounts, including a 1998 Kunming incident where Han Jianwei, visiting a family tomb with family members, filmed an object morphing from a bright ball with something like "two pieces of black rubber" at the top and bottom into a diamond-shaped formation of nine luminous points. [14]

Next, we have two pieces that evoke contemporary alien abduction tales: "**Guests from the Sky**" and "**An Object in the Woods.**"

"Guests from the Sky," which as previously mentioned first led us down the UAP rabbit hole, presents Ji Yun's disturbing account of his close friend Shen Tiechan, another high-ranking Qing dynasty political figure. The story, cobbled together from letters Ji Yun received from Tiechan and testimony from mutual acquaintances, is this: Tiechan, returning from a mountain hunt, encounters two luminous spheres silently tracking him.

Female beings, whom Tiechan believes to be "immortals," descend and transport him inside one of the spheres. There, their strange, otherworldly mistress attempts seduction. [15] A terrified Tiechan initially resists but during a subsequent abduction, surrenders. This seals his fate. Meetings follow, in both dreams and waking life, progressively altering him physically and mentally, until his untimely death.

This carnal dalliance echoes stories of intimate contact between humans and non-human entities that can be found in nearly every culture and age. [16] But more significantly, it prefigures contemporary alien encounters that are marked by erotic or sexual experiences.

Notable examples include Whitley Strieber's encounters detailed in his 1987 bestseller *Communion*; American painter David Huggins' life-long relationship with a "Grey," as portrayed in the 2017 documentary *Love and Saucers*; Brazilian farmer-turned-lawyer Antônio Vilas-Boas's 1957 account (where his physician documented radiation exposure symptom); South African RAF intelligence officer Elizabeth Klarer's 1958 claims; and Chinese forestry worker Meng Zhaoguo's 1994 experience.

Harvard psychiatrist John Mack documented numerous similar accounts from both male and female experiencers in his landmark 1994 work *Abduction: Human Encounters with Aliens*. And more recently, such phenomena were documented in the Department of Defense's 2010 study "Anomalous Acute and Subacute Field Effects on Human and Biological Tissues." This Pentagon report is part of a haul of 1,574 pages of documents obtained by *The Sun* through a Freedom of Information Act legal battle. Compiled by Dr. Christopher Green, professor in Forensic Neuroimaging at Wayne State School of Medicine, it catalogs dozens of U.S. military personnel who suffered severe medical conditions following UAP encounters. Injuries ranged from radiation burns to severe brain damage—effects consistently noted as well by former Pentagon AATIP director Luis Elizondo, who has remarked on pilots returning with unexplained burns, neurological trauma, and incidents of missing time.

Adding a further layer, Dr. Garry Nolan, a Stanford University professor of pathology and renowned immunologist, conducted independent research at the request of CIA officials and aerospace companies. Nolan's work examined approximately 100 government personnel with anomalous health incidents, a subset of whom reported direct UAP encounters resulting in devastating trauma, including radiation-like burns and neurological damage. In public statements and interviews, Nolan has revealed that, among the group he studied, as many as one-quarter ultimately died following their injuries.

These aren't isolated incidents. Civilians across decades and continents report identical injuries: Cohen and Small's "sunburn," Vilas-Boas's radiation sickness (complete with skin lesions, crushing weakness, nausea, and splitting headaches). These modern cases also cast new light on Tiechan's 18th-century symptoms: what seems like brain injury manifesting as impaired communication and a shattered personality so severe that Ji Yun is moved to carefully document it. Ultimately, as with modern cases, Tiechan's condition progresses into a wasting illness characterized by severe vomiting and then death. [17]

The final historical account we'll discuss in depth is the 1880 **"An Object in the Woods."** Although it features no explicit encounters with strange beings, it nevertheless contains virtually every other element of modern abduction narratives. The witness, a peasant named Tan, encounters a floating anomalous object radiating bright polychromatic light in the middle of the woods. As he approaches, paralysis instantly overtakes him, accompanied by profound mental fog. Then comes the most alarming element: Tan finds himself involuntarily levitating skyward.

Soon after, Tan loses consciousness. When awareness returns, Tan finds himself crashing gently through foliage onto an unfamiliar mountainside. After seeking assistance from locals, he discovers that he is inexplicably more than a thousand li, over 300 miles, from home. Contemporary UAP abductions feature identical elements: sudden paralysis, involuntary levitation, anomalous luminous objects, missing time, and waking up far from home.

To fully appreciate the continuity between ancient and modern accounts, let's review a few contemporary Western cases, starting with a mass UFO encounter that rocked Berkshire County, Massachusetts on Sept 1, 1969.

The event, as documented contemporaneously in multiple sources, including the *Berkshire Eagle* newspaper and WSBS radio broadcasts, triggered a flood of emergency calls to the Berkshire police and media throughout the night as over 250 residents independently reported UAP encounters and abduction experiences.

Among them was the Reed family. They came across two luminous orbs that sporadically emitted beams of light, accompanied by a classic disc-shaped craft. They then lost three hours they couldn't account for. When they regained awareness, several family members retained fragmented memories of medical examinations in an enormous chamber resembling a ship's hull. And, unsettlingly, the mother, who had been driving, and the grandmother, who didn't drive, had inexplicably switched seats.

Two other Berkshire residents, Melanie Kirchdorfer and Tom Warner, independently provided corroborating testimony without prior communication with each other or the Reed family. Both described being immobilized in luminous beams, levitated skyward, and experiencing missing time before being delicately deposited back to earth—each at locations miles from where their experiences began.

Another example comes from Nobel Prize-winning chemist

Kary Mullis, who received the 1993 Nobel Prize in Chemistry for developing the polymerase chain reaction (PCR). In his collection of autobiographical essays, *Dancing Naked in the Mind Field*, he recounts how he and his daughter Louise separately experienced missing time episodes near his northern California cabin.

While Mullis' incident includes a bizarre screen memory of a talking, glowing raccoon—"Later, I wondered if it could have been a hologram, projected from God knows where"—and his daughter's features her fiancé frantically looking for her in the woods all night, their core experiences align: a UAP encounter, missing time, and transplantation to a different location.

Significantly, in follow-up interviews, Mullis confided to investigator Bill Chalker that neighbors in the area reported similar strange phenomena—a tiny luminous humanoid that morphed into a full-sized one, and another glowing raccoon.

All of this is extremely bizarre, to say the least. In this, it echoes observations by information scientist Jacques Vallée and philosopher Bernardo Kastrup that bizarreness isn't peripheral but fundamental to UAP encounters and that this says as much about the nature of human perception as it does about the phenomena themselves. [18] Too, it invites us to reconsider the talking animals that populate indigenous traditions and global folklore as perhaps something more than useful metaphors.

Mullis concludes in *Dancing Naked in the Mindfield*, "I wouldn't try to publish a scientific paper about these things because I can't do any experiments. I can't make glowing raccoons appear. I can't buy them from a scientific supply house to study. I can't cause myself to be lost again for several hours. But I don't deny what happened. It's what science calls anecdotal, because it only happened in a way that you can't reproduce. But it happened."

According to historians and witnesses, the ancient accounts discussed here happened too, as did other classical and modern testimonies in the "Sightings" section. Yet vast bodies of accounts remain unrecorded. Comment sections beneath UAP news stories frequently reveal readers' previously untold experiences, kept private for decades due to fear of ridicule or loss of credibility. These testimonials frequently come from individuals identifying themselves as scientists, military personnel, physicians, and other high-credibility professionals who have more to lose than gain by sharing their experiences.

But this silence is starting to break. In 2015, NASA funded a study at Princeton University in which theologians explored how world religions might respond to the existence of aliens, suggesting institutions might be quietly preparing for possibilities they once dismissed. In a similar vein, a 2023 University of Virginia survey found that nearly one in five academics report UAP encounters, either personally or through someone close. Many offered unprompted, strikingly detailed accounts. And dozens of scholars now deep dive into UAP research—from Dr. Diana Pasulka at UNC to Dr. Tim Maudlin of NYU and Dr. Rudolph Schild of the Harvard-Smithsonian Center for Astrophysics. From theological prep work to academic witness testimony, the academic landscape is beginning to shift, buckle, and become delightfully strange.

Far thornier is the problem of disinformation. Gideon Lewis-Kraus's 2021 *New Yorker* article, "How the Pentagon Started Taking U.F.O.s Seriously," details how skepticism about UAP encounters was intentionally reinforced through systematic government suppression spanning decades.

Vice Admiral Roscoe Hillenkoetter, the first CIA Director, for example, confessed in 1960: "Behind the scenes, high-ranking Air Force officers are soberly concerned about UFOs. But through official secrecy and ridicule, many citizens are led to believe the unknown flying objects are nonsense. [19]

Valid reasons may exist to downplay such accounts—

preventing ontological shock, protecting classified projects (or avoiding argument with one's mom about the exact nature of the star that the three wisemen followed). Yet not to boldly go into this territory seems a mistake, especially given the similarities between modern and ancient accounts across the globe. Taken together, they demand we rethink assumptions, including the comfortable fiction that reality is a perfect fit for our worldview and biases. As Ji Yun observed in 1800, those who insist all principles of existence have been discovered are simply being ridiculous.

Despite contemporary problems of transparency and witness gaslighting, we believe the cases and lore in *Stars That Pause*, spanning nearly two millennia and multiple cultures, are enough to compel us to resist dismissing all strange things in the sky as drones or classified projects. Such things have been with us for a long time. Whatever they, and we, might ultimately be.

PART III
RABBIT HOLES

Of course, there are strange things in this world of ours for which there is not yet a theory. As for those who insist all principles of existence have been discovered, and that all phenomena have been recorded, come now, they are simply being ridiculous.

—Ji Yun, Investigator of the Strange

1. EXTRAORDINARY CLAIMS AND BOGGLE THRESHOLDS

"Extraordinary claims require extraordinary evidence." It sounds reasonable enough. But figuring out what actually counts as "extraordinary" is trickier than it appears.

After all, science itself is full of claims that stretch the imagination. In microbiology, we have discovered that what we call a "human body" is essentially a walking rainforest of 30–40 trillion human cells alongside trillions of microflora and microfauna, all working in concert. These microbes influence everything from immunity to mood. Even what seems solid, including ourselves, turns out to be, no matter how much time we spend at the gym, 99.9999999999999% empty space. The sensation of solidity is nothing more than electrostatic repulsion between atoms. These atoms then dissolve upon further scrutiny into mathematical abstractions and shifting energy fields rather than anything we would recognize as matter or "Mother." And in *Wednesday Is Indigo Blue*, neurologists Richard Cytowic and David Eagleman show that people with synesthesia truly experience a different reality—processing senses in ways most

77

of us can scarcely imagine. Wednesdays may appear blue, and shapes can have flavor.

Such claims would have been considered beyond bizarre a century ago. But time has a way of transforming today's fringe ideas into tomorrow's textbook material.

Moreover, what counts as "extraordinary" varies dramatically across cultures. The worldviews of Japanese Shinto environmentalists vs. Indian Hindu philosopher-mathematicians vs. an atheist car mechanic from small-town Kentucky, like our cousin Eddie, are quite different. And what gets pathologized in Euro-Western contexts, such as hearing the voices of ancestors, could be valorized in Northern Plains tribes or certain Asian communities. These worldviews shape not just what people believe but what counts as strong evidence in the first place.

Beyond cultural variation, there's individual variation too. Historian Renée Haynes brilliantly captured this with her concept of the "boggle threshold"—a psychological line separating what we find plausible from what we deem absurd. Haynes defined it specifically as "the level above which the [individual] mind boggles when faced with some new fact, report, or idea."

Haynes herself was comfortable with telepathy, somewhat uncertain about reincarnation, but found it ridiculous that a woman would travel across the world to have her torn aura repaired by a spiritual expert. Another person might embrace the idea of auras but find the idea of the Tao or depth psychology highly suspect. A third might be convinced by Einstein's block theory of time but find the idea of plant intelligence silly.

Such variations are shaped by personal experiences, cultural background, and educational history. Someone who grew up in a household where traditional Chinese medicine was practiced, especially if it proved beneficial, might readily accept the concept of qi energy pathways, while being deeply skeptical of psychiatric medications or Western medical protocols. Similarly, a person who had a powerful mystical experience in their youth might maintain a higher threshold for supernatural phenomena than someone who's only encountered such ideas through books or TikTok testimonials.

Boggle thresholds are essential to our sense of safety and security in the world. Cross them, and people react with sudden, sometimes startling intensity—a reminder of how deeply these boundaries matter. In college classrooms, this happens so frequently that we professors spend considerable time thinking about how to broach issues that might cross students' boggle thresholds: whether they involve the physics of time, animal intelligence, or concepts related to religion, history, or sociology. Yet we encounter these "boggle thresholds" everywhere, along with the intense reactions to them being violated. At dinner parties, on social media, during grocery store conversations—anytime a topic threatens our underlying worldview. But once you know what you're looking at, those heated reactions become less mysterious.

Zhou Dunyi's Taijitu
周敦颐太极图

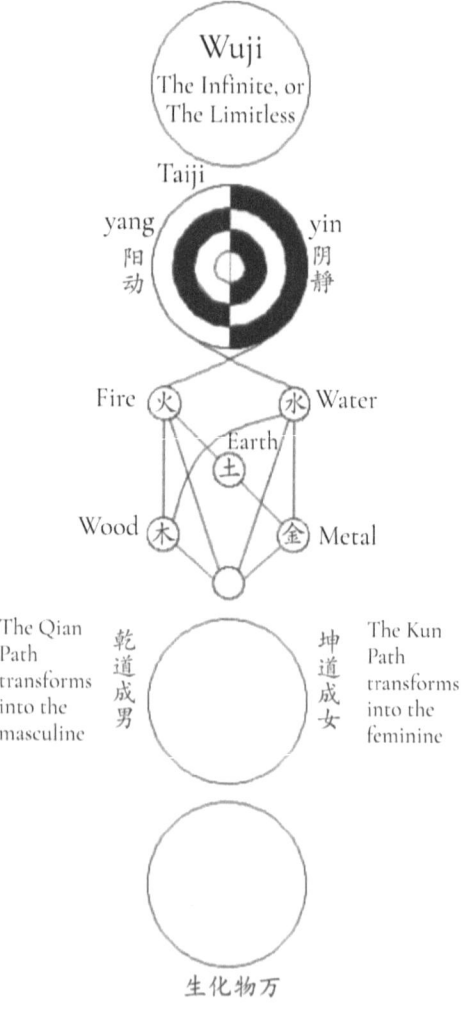

Generation and transformation of the ten thousand things

2. CHINESE UFO THEORY

While Erich von Däniken's *Chariots of the Gods* was capturing Western imaginations in the 1970s, China too got in the game. As the shadows of the Cultural Revolution lifted, an intellectual renaissance took root, and Chinese researchers offered approaches to UFOs steeped in classical texts, mythology, and philosophy. This potent combination gained support from figures like Qian Xuesen, the "father of China's space program," and produced visionary theorists over the next several decades.

Among them was Lin Qingquan, whose 1993 book *Eastern UFOlogy* became the purest crystallization of what some called "Qigong UFOlogy," a distinctly Chinese blend of metaphysical principles with Western mathematical formalization that was shaped by Lin's educational background in astrophysics and *I Ching* studies. Lin argued that flying saucers operated through principles found in classical texts like the *I Ching*. Specifically, he proposed:

Yin Flight [隐飞行]

UAP propulsion, Lin claimed, relies on "yin" (hidden, secret) flight, an ability also attributed to Taoist and qigong masters, allowing material bodies to shift at the speed of thought between full (实) and empty (虚) forms, or between the visibly manifest (显) and the nowhere-to-be-found hidden (隐), like clouds gathering and dissolving. This shifting is analogous to toggling between the quantum and Newtonian worlds, as if one is downshifting from a field of possibilities into a single material actualization or shifting from energy to matter. In this way, energetic unity is not opposed to the material, but is its underlying truth, just as our bodies are simultaneously swarms of orbiting atoms and also undeniably "us," enjoying a meal at the all-you-can-eat Korean barbecue buffet.

It is exactly this metaphysical duality that enables bilocation, sudden invisibility, instantaneous travel, and the creation of objects from pure thought, as seen in both traditional tales and historical records of spiritual feats.

At the heart of this philosophical line of thought lies the concept of "hua" (化)—transformation as a fundamental cosmic process—and its sibling concept, "hua shen" (化身), which describes how celestial beings transform their bodies at will.

Unlike the default Western belief in stable materiality, "hua" teaches everything is in flux: cells renew in the human body as we daily digest other life forms and transform them into ourselves, seeds grow into plants, plants become oil and gas, weather and seasons cycle, products of the imagination become realities, and new personalities emerge as we fall into conversation with different people in different places—and as our consciousness takes on a dizzying variety of forms nightly in our dreams. Likewise, in the natural world, clownfish and wrasse fish change sex; axolotls regrow limbs, brains, and hearts; and starfish reconstitute themselves from fragments. Even human existence begins as a twinkle in our parents' eyes, then a surreal otherworldly meet-up between a tadpole-like sperm and a mystical oval egg, which morphs into an unfolding process that looks like a fast-forward of humanity's entire evolution.

Taiji Compass Navigation [太极罗盘]

Lin also proposed that the non-human intelligence behind UAPs might use some type of "Taiji compass" to navigate via channeling qi—the vital cosmic energy produced by the dynamic interplay of yin and yang and which underlies all reality, like the ocean gives rise to waves.

This techno-shamanic device is inspired by a real instrument: the Luo Pan, used by feng shui practitioners. Like a regular compass, the Luo Pan's needle responds to magnetic forces. But unlike ordinary compasses, its center is surrounded by 5 to 52 concentric rings inscribed with the Eight Trigrams (basic patterns of change in the universe), the Five Elements (fundamental forces that shape the world), and symbols reflecting celestial time cycles. Masters read where the Luo Pan needle falls in relation to these rings to figure out which locations are suitable for particular activities, where luck pools or tragedy awaits, and what times are auspicious for building.

Essentially, the Luo Pan "reads" frequencies and qualities of both physical and spiritual energy—each a facet of qi—to discover useful nexus points where energies overlap. Reading it is a fine art, like other forms of divination, and the needle can tremble, bob, or flicker in response to invisible forces in our interconnected world extending well beyond the magnetic. Those forces might be connected to physical things underground (old bones, wells, veins of iron), the aftershocks of ancient events (rituals, deaths, births), or astrological data like planetary alignments and birth time.

This tradition is still very much alive in places like mainland China, Hong Kong, and Taiwan. And major corporations regularly consult Luo Pan specialists before erecting a skyscraper or launching a new marketing initiative, just as American financial brokerages still make use of astrologers in addition to fundamental and technical stock analysts.

Simultaneously occult and technological, it empowers users to work with natural law rather than against it and locates shortcuts through spacetime that enable ships to leap immense distances instantaneously as well as travel forwards and backwards in time. In this way, it reflects the parable of Cook Ding who learned to cut with the natural lines of meat so well that it would fall apart with the barest of cuts, and Zhuangzi's parable of the fish, where swimming fish show how to move with the Tao: using the current instead of battling it.

Thought Engines [意念力]

Regarding how such travel is possible, Lin explained that spiritual thought itself is the ultimate tool. According to Lin, focused mental force—consciousness attuned and released with intention by the pilot—manipulates the craft's internal information state to unstick it from regular spacetime—just as our thoughts move our bodies. Again, it's useful to think of this as flipping between quantum and Newtonian states, or conversely, between yin and yang realms (阴阳交变). All elements other than thought—compasses, meditative skills, even advanced alien hardware—simply serve to direct, shape, interface with, or amplify consciousness. Ultimately, everything comes down to transforming and deploying the mind's innate potential and the wider field of consciousness it's part of.

Qi [气] Absorption

Lin also speculated that alien beings, like Earth's qigong masters, directly absorb "qi," eliminating their need for food and clothing, and making them impervious to temperature and nearly immortal to boot.

Downloading

How did Lin Qingquan receive these insights?

That highlights another interesting aspect of Chinese UFO theories. Specifically, he claimed that his insights were downloaded or channeled during states of deep meditation, directly from some mysterious source.

This process echoes advanced qigong practice, where mastery grants purported access to universal intelligence; descriptions by Chinese Daoist sages of visionary trances in which they received new knowledge; Indian yogic traditions that speak of "śruti" or revealed wisdom, sometimes arriving intact in meditation and yogic practices; or Buddhist traditions that likewise detail the spontaneous appearance of "siddhis"—special insights or powers gifted from concentrated meditation and spiritual practice.

Such claims intersect with the broader Chinese metaphysical tradition, where revelation, trance, and intuitive knowledge are highly prized as legitimate sources of insight. But as well they resonate with Western traditions and cases, several of which Dr. Diana Walsh Pasulka explores in her 2019 *American Cosmic* and 2023 *Encounters*. Here, Pasulka documents how contemporary scientists, engineers, and experiencers sometimes describe suddenly receiving insights, visions, or entire blueprints from seemingly external or nonhuman sources. She especially highlights central figures in the Russian and American space programs, such as Konstantin Tsiolkovsky and Jack Parsons, who ritualistically reported receiving downloads from higher intelligences or nonhuman minds.

Experiences of knowledge being received or downloaded span both Western and Eastern creative traditions, ranging from visits from the muse to more dramatic accounts of divine intervention. Essential parts of René Descartes' rational philosophy, which ironically laid the foundations for science and epistemology, came through angelic visits in his dreams. And Nikola Tesla claimed he received, while awake, the ideas for his inventions from an external source along with signals from intelligences beyond Earth.

Ancient Astronaut Theories

Chinese researchers also shared other important aspects in common with Western UFO theorists, particularly ancient astronaut theories. Like their counterparts, they identified enigmatic artifacts as potential evidence of alien presence. This includes the Sanxingdui bronze masks with their distinctive "alien" features, unusual "helmeted" humanoid figures in Ningxia petroglyphs, and the shamanically surreal 4,000-year-old Kangjiashimenzi petroglyphs. In this tableau, which at first glance appears to be a fertility-themed and tantalizingly inclusive orgy, theorists find evidence of alien-human hybridization—pointing to the figures' antennae-like features, the numerous flying face-orbs depicted among the human figures, and the organized, ritualistic nature of the sexual activity as suggesting extraterrestrial genetic experimentation.

They also sometimes reinterpreted ancient Chinese texts through the lens of extraterrestrial contact. For example, the Yellow Emperor (Huangdi), one of China's legendary founding rulers, was seen as a potential extraterrestrial visitor, while his mythical dragon flights between earth and heaven became spacecraft journeys. China's first emperor, Qin Shi Huang, possessed a special mirror said to reveal internal organs, which to some suggested advanced medical scanning technology; meanwhile, *The Classic of Mountains and Seas* (compiled roughly between 4th century BCE and 1st century BCE), with its accounts of unusual beings and flying vehicles, assumed new significance. So too did inventories of strange beings and strange vehicles in other traditions, such as the *Drona Parva* sections of the ancient Indian Sanskrit epic *Mahabharata*, which describe vimanas—self-luminous aerial craft capable of hovering and rapid directional changes, and equipped with weapons producing blinding light and effects that some modern readers liken to radiation sickness.

Purpose and Method

It is not just content that distinguishes the Chinese tradition. It is also purpose and method.

As philosopher and writer Lin Yutang observed in the 1940s, Western thought can sometimes overemphasize "the approach of facts," obsessively documenting data while ignoring larger questions of meaning and relationship. He contrasted this with what he called the Chinese "approach of values," which stresses implications for human consciousness and our relationship with reality. Chinese thought also works harder to contextualize present conversations within larger historical trajectories, deeper philosophical frameworks, and embodied existence in the world, as well as to look for opportunities for self-cultivation and living in harmony with all aspects of reality—whether visible or hidden.

This integration, moreover, reflects other important aspects of the Chinese approach. First, there is what philosopher Fung

Yu-Lan, one of 20th-century China's leading scholars, identified as perhaps the most distinctive characteristic of Chinese thought: an ability to be "this-worldly and other-worldly" at the same time. The ideal human being aims to achieve both "sageliness within" and "kingliness without": to cultivate spiritual wisdom internally while effectively engaging with the wider world and taking on meaningful roles in society.

This approach recognizes that understanding phenomena requires both empirical observation and the cultivation of deeper perception and does not see an interest in metaphysical or spiritual phenomena as opposed to occupying high-status scientific, business, or intellectual positions. It is also typical of Eastern thought's tendency to move beyond the either/or (A or not A) structure of Aristotelian logic and embrace both/and logic, where multiple perspectives or theories can both be partially true.

A final related element is how the East Asian tradition seeks to understand abstract or exotic concepts through concrete, everyday experiences, such as observing how trees move in the wind. Rather than seeing phenomena like UFOs as separate from practical concerns or everyday matters, it assumes everything is interconnected. Insight in one domain can illuminate another. Indeed, the key to understanding the elusive phenomena is by diving much more deeply into our ordinary world so that it becomes extraordinary. This is something we've tried to do in our modest way throughout this book.

3. UFOS, UAPS, AND WTFS: THE MAGIC OF NAMES

The term "UAP," originally an abbreviation for unidentified aerial phenomena but then changed to unidentified anomalous phenomena, has increasingly overtaken "UFO" as the label of choice in recent years. On one hand, this is simple image rehabilitation: just as "comic books" became "graphic literature," and fantasy was recast as "speculative fiction." Likewise, sweetbreads and Rocky Mountain oysters acquired genteel names to placate the squeamish.

Renaming is a powerful cognitive tool. It shakes off old prejudices and invites new interpretations. This is implicitly understood by teenagers who adopt nicknames, hip-hop artists who take up alter egos, bureaucrats who reduce people to numbers, and farm workers who insist a cow's name should be "cow" rather than "Beth." In fact, when the Pentagon officially adopted "UAP" in 2020, media coverage shifted almost overnight: out went the "little green men" jokes, in came sober talk of national security.

But this term shift also importantly acknowledges that many

"UFO" accounts in fact depict objects transitioning between aerial and underwater environments—like the shell-shaped craft in our 1899 account—or objects that are entirely aquatic USOs (unidentified submersible objects). And "flying" is simply way too reductive a verb for the specific ways some of these things seem to defy the laws of physics. Most significantly though, this linguistic pivot brings attention to the bizarre overlap between what once seemed like entirely separate classes of anomalies. That recognition has become a focal point in UAP studies thanks to the persistent work of researchers.

Among the most recent and methodical researchers is Rey Hernandez. A federal tax attorney by profession, Hernandez was a committed disbeliever in the paranormal until he and his family experienced it firsthand (as discussed further in Rabbit Hole 14). Subsequently, he co-founded the Foundation for Research into Extraterrestrial and Extraordinary Experiences (FREE) with Apollo 14 astronaut Dr. Edgar Mitchell, Harvard astrophysicist Dr. Rudy Schild, and researcher Mary Rodwell.

Starting in 2013, Hernandez and his team led a landmark study that surveyed more than 4,000 people from over 100 countries who reported encounters with non-human intelligences. These included everything from UAP sightings and near-death experiences to poltergeists and other extraordinary phenomena.

The research combined comprehensive quantitative questionnaires with open-ended questions that invited rich qualitative narratives. Unlike many previous investigations, participants were instructed to report only conscious, explicit memories—no hypnosis, dreams, or channeled material. The aim was to ensure the data's integrity and preempt kneejerk disbelief.

The eye-opening findings revealed common ground shared

across a wide spectrum of weirdness. This included telepathic communication (reported by 78% of respondents), profound shifts in perception of time and space, encounters with beings perceived as interdimensional rather than merely extraterrestrial, healing phenomena (reported by 50% of respondents), and consciousness-expanding effects similar to those described in mystical and shamanic traditions.

Other scholars like Peter Rojcewicz, Jacques Vallée (*Passport to Magonia*), and John Keel (*The Mothman Prophecies*) have found similar patterns to the FREE study. Dr. Peter Rojcewicz, a folklore specialist, has written extensively on the parallels between UAP encounters and accounts of fairies, djinn, angels, and other supernatural beings. All frequently involve missing time, telepathic communication, and altered states of consciousness. Jacques Vallée—the French-American astrophysicist and computer scientist who helped develop the early internet and served as Spielberg's model for the French researcher in *Close Encounters of the Third Kind*—demonstrates too in *Passport to Magonia* how centuries-old tales of fairy abductions mirror modern alien abduction accounts, down to details like paralysis and missing time.

Likewise, the investigations of John Keel reveal how high-strangeness events (poltergeist activity, men in black encounters, cryptid sightings) overlap and cluster around certain UAP hotspots. These include the Skinwalker Ranch in Utah, the Hoia Baciu forest in Romania, and the Sai Kung peninsula in southern China—an alleged "barrier" zone and longstanding UFO hotspot along Hong Kong's MacLehose Trail, where hiker reports include classic "Oz-effect" silences, sudden storm anomalies, missing-time episodes, and encounters with faceless shadow figures and other entities.

This growing body of research challenges the view that UAPs

are simply alien "nuts and bolts" spacecraft from other planets. Instead, it suggests a more complex, consciousness-related interaction—one that spans dimensions and realities, defying the neat classification systems we have historically tried to impose on the strange.

4. THE TAO OF JUNG

A few years back, the psychologist Carl Jung had almost entirely vanished from American university reading lists, when suddenly we noticed students talking about him again. Curious, we investigated, and that's when we found out that not only had the K-pop group BTS launched a series of albums based on his concepts of persona, ego, and shadow, but that these were in turn inspired by Murray Stein's South Korean bestseller, *Jung's Map of the Soul*. This new wave of interest in Jung wasn't confined to South Korea. In fact, while his psychology had been largely exiled from American universities, it had been blossoming across Asia.

Japanese anime like Chiaki J. Konaka's *Serial Experiments Lain* (1998) and *Ghost Hound* (2007) explicitly wove Jungian references into their storylines and dialogue, exploring both virtual and astral realities. Jung-focused institutes in Asia fused art, meditation, and psychoanalysis into vibrant interdisciplinary communities. In Chinese science fiction, stories like Chen Qiufan's "A History of Future Illnesses" discussed Jung's psychological ideas in relation to Taoism, role set theory, and the inhabitation of multiple avatars—quoting memorable lines from Carl Jung himself, such as: "I simply believe that some part of the human Self or Soul is not subject to the laws of space and time."

This deep cultural impact makes Jung an essential reference point not just for anyone interested in Asian culture, but especially for those drawn to the speculative or paranormal traditions that animate it. In fact, Jung's work demonstrates a profound engagement with (and debt owed to) Taoist principles.

Central to understanding this is recognizing how correlative thinking, fundamental to the Asian worldview via classical Chinese thought, permeates his entire psychological theory. Unlike the West's almost exclusive focus on direct cause-effect relationships, Chinese thought equally emphasizes systematic, and frequently fractal, correspondences. These ripple across harmonizing orders of reality: human, natural, and divine; psychological, physical, and social; macro and micro—each like a tuning fork resonating with deeper primordial principles. Indeed, Sinologists Joseph Needham and Benjamin Schwartz argue that musical harmony offers the best metaphor for understanding correlative thinking.

This correlative worldview fundamentally shaped many of Jung's most important ideas, particularly the following:

Synchronicity

Jung defined synchronicity as meaningful coincidences between mental and physical events that cannot be explained by cause and effect. His most famous example involves a patient describing a dream about a golden scarab beetle, when at that very moment, a real scarab beetle tapped against Jung's window —the psychic and physical worlds intermingling in meaningful connection.

Synchronicity draws directly from the Chinese idea of "ganying" (resonance). Jung explicitly acknowledged this influence in a 1930 speech later included in his foreword to Richard Wilhelm's translation of the *I Ching*, the classic Chinese manual of divination. "The science of the *I Ching* is not based on the causality principle, but on a principle [. . .] which I have tentatively called the synchronistic principle," Jung writes, adding that "The ancient Chinese mind contemplates the cosmos in a way comparable to that of the modern [quantum] physicist, who cannot deny that his model of the world is a decidedly psychophysical structure"(24). Jung's quantum physics comparison here is no throw-away bit of "woo"-ery. It speaks directly to interpretations of quantum physics that suggest consciousness and matter are interconnected at a fundamental level. And he developed the concept in close dialogue with the pioneering and Nobel Prize-winning quantum physicist Wolfgang Pauli. In 1952, they even published a collection exploring the relationship between psyche and matter, *The Interpretation of Nature and the Psyche*.

Jung's fidelity to this psychophysical worldview led to him adopting a position of dual-aspect monism. This is to say that he believed psyche and matter are two different manifestations or frequencies of the same underlying unified reality. Similarly, the Tao is regarded as the ultimate ground of all existence, an undivided whole that gives rise to both subjective (mental) and objective (material) experiences as well as time/space and other foundational categories.

Archetypes and Li

Very closely related to Jung's theory of synchronicity is his theory of archetypes. Archetypes are innate universal patterns and images residing in the collective unconscious (a sort of mass consciousness field) shared by all human beings and that manifest across cultures in dreams, myths, literature, art, and human behavior as organizing principles of psychological experience. Much like Plato's theory of forms (which also influenced Jung), these archetypes can influence physical matter since they are basically "psychoid" factors. This means they are neither purely psychic nor purely physical but lie in an underlying "meta" domain where psyche and matter are undifferentiated and from which both proceed. Here, Jung's theory of archetypes closely parallels not only his thoughts on synchronicity but also the Chinese concept of "li," the basic organizing cosmic principles that pattern fundamental reality and that connect all things.

Anima and Animus

In Taoism, yin and yang famously represent the fundamental dualities of existence, opposing but interconnected forces that shape the natural world. Rather than fixed opposites, they exist in a constant state of change. This is to say that they continuously flow into one another as part of a larger equilibrium—just as winter gives way to spring and night leads into day, bear markets lead into bulls, each containing the seed of the other.

Traditionally, yin is associated with the feminine—darkness, receptivity, and intuition—while yang represents the masculine—light, activity, and reason, although the terms "feminine" and "masculine" mean something much more fundamental than gender identity which is itself an expression of these forces. In keeping with their interconnected nature, these distinctions are not absolute nor are they statically binary; rather, they reflect a dynamic relationship, where each depends on the other to maintain balance. Taoism ultimately emphasizes that true harmony is not about opposition but about recognizing and aligning with this natural rhythm.

Fascinated by this approach, Jung drew heavily upon yin/yang interplay and their broader context to develop his ideas about the "anima" and "animus," the female and male principles that Jung believed exist within everyone's psyche. He maintained that psychological wholeness requires integrating these complementary forces, rather than reinforcing strict binaries. Men must acknowledge their inner feminine principle (anima), while women must recognize their inner masculine principle (animus).

Jung discusses the influence of yin/yang principles on his psychology in several works spanning decades—from his 1929 commentary on *The Secret of the Golden Flower* (a Taoist meditation text translated by Richard Wilhelm), through *Alchemical Studies* and *Archetypes and the Collective Unconscious*, and prominently in *Psychological Types*.

Jung writes, for example, in *Psychological Types*: "Yang signifies warmth, light, maleness; yin is cold, darkness, femaleness [. . .]. As a microcosm, man [a human being] is a reconciler of the opposites"(216–17). Jung goes on here to identify the conscious mind with yang qualities and the unconscious with yin qualities. And just as Taoist practice seeks harmony through balancing these opposing forces, Jung's therapeutic focus is on harmonizing these fundamental patterns within ourselves.

Jung, UFOs, and Things That Go Bump in the Mind

These theories of complementary opposites and psychophysical unity provided Jung with an insightful way to approach phenomena that blur the boundaries of mind and matter. For instance, tulpas are thought forms in Tibetan mysticism that allegedly gain physical existence through intense visualization, and poltergeists are psychokinetic manifestations of unconscious psychological energies. Jung even applied these concepts specifically to UFOs in his 1959 *Flying Saucers: A Modern Myth of Things Seen in the Skies*, where he suggests that they represent archetypes from the collective unconscious manifesting in physical reality, hints of a path to wholeness and spiritual cultivation in an age of mass anxiety.

In articulating this, Jung fundamentally shifted the conversation about UFOs from merely conceiving them as physical craft from outer space to understanding them as psychic phenomena with physical manifestations, an interpretive framework that continues as one of the main schools of thought in contemporary ufology.

5. CONFESSIONS OF WILD GODS

What do you do when your worldview doesn't allow for the paranormal, but you experience a phenomenon that doesn't fit comfortably in with what you thought you knew about the world either?

Barbara Ehrenreich's 2014 memoir *Living with a Wild God* offers a fascinating case study for just this situation. In it, you have an atheist intellectual with impeccable scientific credentials (a PhD in Cellular Immunology) grappling with an unexplained phenomenon. Before this memoir, Ehrenreich, an investigative journalist and professor, was best known for her 2001 *Nickel and Dimed: On (Not) Getting by in America*. It chronicled her experience working undercover in low-wage jobs. But in *Living with a Wild God*, she recounts something very different from her usual sociological interests: a profound mystical encounter from her teenage years during which everything appeared aflame with light, and she experienced a "presence" that felt radically "other."

Ehrenreich struggled for decades to both forget and make sense of this experience. But even when she finally decided to write a book about it, rather than embracing a supernatural explanation, she hypothesized the existence of an unknown species—in keeping with her training.

This method, accepting the reality of an experience while staying open to multiple, non-default explanations, is a model for grappling with not just the strange but any experience. It can equally put the brakes on specious or knee-jerk sociological, historical, or psychological explanations which sometimes get thrown around like ninja stars. And it's something exhibited by high-caliber intellectuals across time and culture. For example, Ji Yun, who inspired our book, also consistently offers multiple interpretations, including psychological or physical explanations, for the strange accounts he discusses, showing a degree of intellectual humility that commonly marks Chinese writing.

But there's another important way in which Ehrenreich invokes Ji Yun. It's another important aspect to consider when making sense of the paranormal accounts of others. That's the fact that many people wait until late life to share these accounts. Ehrenreich certainly did, admitting freely she did so to avoid the social stigma. Ji Yun likewise waited until his later years. They are not alone in waiting decades to speak—butting against the common belief that people are eager to make up strange things and share them in a bid to "get attention," as is often claimed.

In fact, this pattern of delayed disclosure, keeping extraordinary experiences secret until late in life, appears across many different types of anomalous encounters, from mystical experiences to UAP sightings, just as it occurs in regard to confessions about secret affairs, crimes, or regrets. This only makes sense. Late life is often marked by a release from the social and professional constraints that might have previously discouraged disclosure, accompanied too by a desire for courageous truth-telling and unburdening.

In *The Top Five Regrets of the Dying*, hospice nurse Bronnie

Ware discusses asking her dying patients what they regretted most about their lives. One of the most common things they admitted was that they wished they had the courage to live a life true to themselves, not the life others expected of them, and the courage to express their feelings. This is a potent combination for the confessional urge. And it makes sense of the large variety of retirement-age or deathbed confessions in relation to UAP experiences.

Nat Kobitz, the US Navy's former longtime Director of Science and Technology Development, for example, only discussed classified UFO programs when he was 92 years old and dying from cancer. According to investigative journalist Ross Coulthart, Kobitz admitted he had been read into a classified program involving retrieved nonhuman technology. Similarly, Lieutenant Walter Haut, the press officer at Roswell Army Airfield who issued the original 1947 press release about a "flying disc," signed a sealed affidavit before his death in 2005. In it, he affirmed that his original report was accurate—despite being forced by his superiors to retract it and issue the now-famous "weather balloon" explanation. Haut maintained that he had indeed seen both a UFO crash and alien bodies (details he also shared with his daughter Julie Shuster). Maria Wang made comparable revelations when UFO researcher William Steinman tracked her down in the 1980s. The widow of Dr. Eric Wang, head of the Department of Special Studies at Wright Patterson Air Force Base, claimed that before his death in 1960, her husband had confided to her that the US government was studying recovered extraterrestrial craft.

While these claims may seem dramatic, late-life unburdening is a well-documented phenomenon, even in cases involving seemingly straightforward UAP sightings. One notable example is Lieutenant Colonel Charles Halt, former deputy base commander of a Royal Air Force installation, who waited until after his military career to speak fully about his December 1980 encounter with unidentified aerial phenomena in Rendlesham Forest—an event now considered one of the most thoroughly documented UFO incidents in history.

For those studying anomalous experiences, the voices of older individuals, freed from the social, professional, and reputational constraints of earlier life stages, represent a rich and relatively under-explored source of testimony. And maybe too they can teach us something about the courage to resist closed definitions and fixed ideas.

6. ULTRATERRESTRIALS

The investigative journalist John Keel popularized the ultraterrestrial hypothesis in his 1970 *Operation Trojan Horse*, further elaborating it in *The Eighth Tower*. Unlike the belief that UAPs come from other planets, Keel proposes that these phenomena instead originate from beings who have always inhabited Earth alongside us but exist in a different dimensional plane normally imperceptible to humans.

More specifically, in *The Eighth Tower*, Keel proposes the existence of a "superspectrum," an electromagnetic realm that occasionally intersects with ours, whether by intentional tuning by intelligences on either side, planetary alignment, ritual, geophysical traits, or simply because some places are "thin" for unknown reasons. Supporting this theory, Keel notes in "Secret UFO Bases Across the U.S." that UAPs have been "consistently active in the same areas for many years," suggesting they "originate in some unknown manner from these areas."

Such an idea brings to mind the Buddhist teaching that multiple "lokas," multiple realms of existence, some more malleable than others, all arise from an underlying undetermined emptiness. Thus, what we take as the primary reality, our "material" realm, is neither primary nor all that material but simply one layer of a multi-dimensional reality, at best just a bit more consensual and stable than some others. Consciousness is the primary vehicle for moving between these dimensions—just as throughout our day, we shift mentally between past, present, and future, or slip from sharpened conscious focus to a subconscious stream of thought, or into highway hypnosis or artistic concentration "flow" states in which we lose our "I," or how nightly we slip from waking to dreaming mind or other forms of awareness.

Advanced meditators in the Buddhist tradition are said to develop siddhis—special abilities or powers—that allow them to perceive and interact with beings in different realms. They also become aware that reality is malleable to varying degrees, such as on bardo and imaginal planes that are intensely sensitive to human intention and manifestation.

The ultraterrestrial hypothesis also comes in several non-interdimensional flavors. Some researchers suggest that "aliens" might actually be earth natives (or ancient extraterrestrial colonists): advanced civilizations who've somehow kept themselves hidden for millennia. The world's oceans, given their size and inaccessibility, are prime suspects for such hidden civilizations. Philosopher Michael Glawson, for example, notes that, with at least some UFOs able to travel underwater, and with 70% of the Earth oceanic and 80–95% unexplored—"the idea that these things are from here seems more plausible."

Adding weight to the oceanic hypothesis, a 2024 Sol Foundation white paper, "Beneath the Surface: We May Learn More about UAP by Looking in the Ocean," by Retired Rear Admiral Tim Gallaudet (former head of the National Oceanic and Atmospheric Administration), reviews Navy sightings of "Unidentified Submersible Objects." It describes craft moving at extreme speeds and in impossible ways that far outstrip any known technology, demonstrating the ability to cross seamlessly between air and water, and showing no signs of visible propulsion.

Former Russian Navy officer Vladimir Azhazha has made similar claims, as quoted in Timothy Good's *Unearthly Disclosure*: "Fifty percent of UFO encounters are connected with oceans. Fifteen more—with lakes. So, UFOs tend to stick to the water." To boot, UFO historian Richard Dolan has catalogued aquatic anomalies from around the world, going back centuries, in his recent *A History of USOs*.

Regardless of what one makes of these claims, they overlap fascinatingly with East Asian traditions. Chinese tales, such as those recorded in *The Shadow Book of Ji Yun*, tell of Kunlun Mountain, home to immortals and other supernatural beings. It is ruled by a shaman-like Queen Mother of the West and is only visible to those with "special sight." Korean myth describes Shinshi, a sacred city founded by sky-descended beings atop mist-shrouded Mount Taebaek. And Japanese folklore speaks of the Dragon Palace, a crystal palace beneath the waves where time flows differently and visitors may return home to find centuries have slipped away. There is also Tokoyo no Kuni, a mysterious otherworld that is said to exist across the sea, beneath it, or in a parallel spiritual dimension.

The Japanese tradition is worth zooming in on for a moment since it is heavily influenced by Shintoism, an animistic religious system rooted in shamanism. Shinto envisions the world as a living field, crowded with presences that slip in and out of perception. Especially relevant to our discussion are the kami: neither fixed gods nor simple spirits, but relational agencies—presences that "switch on" when place, time, ritual, mood, and intention align. In other words, kami are more verb and event than noun and substance: like a hand opening from a fist, consciousness flaring up from complexity, or a side of your personality emerging only with certain friends. Once kami surface from the world-soul, they can ensoul a mountain or tree, a crafted object like a teapot, or even a passing storm. Some kami endure for centuries as mountain guardians or shrine spirits; others appear only briefly: on a single "charged" festival night, or while one is gazing up at the sky.

Across Asia, this relational logic recurs. Daoist thought holds that spirit (shen) arises when qi, yin–yang, and the Five Phases harmonize. Zen and Taoist notions of spontaneity and non-duality suggest that when two creators, minds, or environments intersect in just the right way, a third intelligence emerges—irreducible to either alone. This idea surfaces in ancient parables like Zhuangzi's "The Parable of an Axe," as well as in modern formulations such as William S. Burroughs' "The Third Mind," and Tufts University developmental biologist Michael Levin's comment that "right here on Earth, there are already 'aliens' among us that stretch and often break our familiar ways of thinking about Self and Other." For Levin, intelligence is not just a property tied to particular physical forms, but is also an emergent property of persistent, self-organizing patterns, resonating with ancient conceptions of mind that are event-based, relational, and often fleeting.

Such visions of relational, emergent intelligence, whether discussed in contemporary science or ancient spirituality, find echoes in European folklore where the landscapes teem with "fair folk" and "hidden people."

A recent academic study, which has drawn popular attention, brings these connections into sharp focus. The 2024 "Cryptoterrestrial Hypothesis," co-authored by psychologist Tim Lomas, alongside theologian Brendan Case of the Harvard Human Flourishing Program, and biological anthropologist Michael Masters of Montana Technological University, argues that many so-called "alien" encounters may be contact with hidden earthbound intelligences, camouflaged from us by sophisticated technology or techniques for manipulating perception.

Such glamouring is by no means outlandish. It is an extension of cognitive tampering that is already scientifically possible, from the implantation of false memories, the editing of traumatic memories, and group hypnosis to Neuralink brain-to-brain communication that allows monkeys to play Pong with their mind alone and the population of the real world by digital Pokémon—though imagined on a much grander scale. The authors suggest that such perceptual distortion could account for the surreal, bizarre nature of many UAP reports: fragmented, symbol-rich memories, uncanny missing time, and dreamlike aftereffects described by shell-shocked witnesses.

Alternatively, these distortions might simply reflect human minds struggling to process contact with forms and states of being that are radically other. Whether actively manipulated or not, our default cognitive, physiological, and cultural filters after all determine both what we see and how we see it—from our experience of time and space to the taste of things.

This processing challenge is wonderfully illustrated by physicist Michio Kaku's famous analogy on inter-species recognition: if ants in an anthill near a highway encountered a human, they would not comprehend what they're experiencing. They have no concepts for "highway," "car," or "city." The ultraterrestrial hypothesis suggests we might be in a similar position: not just encountering an advanced civilization that has always shared our planet, but one operating with technologies and ideas so far outside our perceptual and cognitive range that we simply can't digest them.

This difficulty reaches to the very basis of what it means to consciously inhabit reality, especially if two beings occupy radically different dimensions of it, whether the vastness of the macrocosmic sea or the intricacies of a microcosmic forest or something far more energetic, relational, or post-biological.

Religious studies scholar Jeffrey Kripal of Rice University, in *Changed in a Flash*, compares our situation in trying to grasp the anomalous to that of an octopus, with its distributed nervous system and alien mode of perception, trying to communicate with humans. And just as we cannot comprehend how an octopus experiences reality despite sharing our world, ultraterrestrials may operate according to perceptual principles and aspects of physics so foreign to our consciousness that their presence registers only as fleeting anomalies at the edges of our awareness. What we're experiencing in confrontations with such phenomena may be, in Kripal's words, a "translation problem" between radically different forms of consciousness (179).

Thus ultimately, ultraterrestrial encounters, and the theories they inspire, are not just encounters with the strange but encounters with the limits of meaning itself and our minds' ability to fully inhabit every dimension of this strange planet that we call home.

7. THE SHADOW BOOK OF JI YUN

Born in 1724, the same year as Immanuel Kant, Ji Yun was a Chinese prodigy who could read by age four. After placing seventh in the national civil service examination, he rose to hold an impressive series of national posts, including Head of the Departments of Public Works, War, and Rites, and Special Advisor to the Emperor. And he did all this while maintaining a reputation as a champion teahouse "free-styler" of poetic couplets.

When the Chinese Emperor Qianlong appointed Ji Yun as Imperial Librarian and had him oversee a massive imperial library project, his national career took a darker turn, however. As chief editor, Ji Yun was ordered to destroy and censor historical accounts that the emperor found ideologically or philosophically distasteful.

When he reached old age, partly in rebellion against this censorship and partly driven by his own strange experiences, Ji Yun (shocking many of his staunchly materialist Confucian colleagues) began writing five volumes of "zhiguai"—"records of the strange"—during his evenings.

The zhiguai genre wasn't new. Stretching back to the Han dynasty (202 BCE–220 CE), these texts had long served as "shadow histories" preserving accounts too unusual for official archives, whether related to science or the paranormal, while also including Buddhist or Taoist philosophical parables meant to awaken readers to metaphysical or spiritual truths. Its inclusivity stemmed from being defined more by psychological impact than subject matter. The classical scholar Hu Gaowang put it this way: "Zhiguai are to be respected because they possess the power to awaken readers to the deep principles of reality. They do this by fixing their attention on that which they previously looked away from, while filling their hearts with fear and awe."

By Ji Yun's time, though, many of his contemporaries had abandoned this classical function and just used the genre to tell wild, entertaining, and completely fictional tales, with no great fidelity to imparting truth. Ji Yun vehemently argued against this. Instead, he adhered to the traditional historian's approach, insisting on recording eyewitness and second-hand accounts whenever possible, including his own experiences, those of family members, friends, and colleagues, and stories he collected across the provinces—all while maintaining a healthy dose of scholarly skepticism.

The result? Five volumes that offer a unique blend of paranormal and travel memoirs, scientific reflections, parables, and early speculative fictions. These volumes combine insights into Chinese science, magic, and metaphysics with a wild array of tales: everything from cannibal villages, sentient fogs, alien encounters, and simulation experiences to observations on early technology, soul swapping, hauntings, reincarnation accounts, divination practices, haunted cities, fox spirits, and tales of Chinese "vampires."

8. CURRENTLY SCREENING: MASS SIGHTINGS OF UFOS AT THE MOVIE THEATERS

Official investigations across multiple countries consistently find a small but significant percentage of reported UAP cases that defy conventional explanation, ranging from 2% to 10%. These often involve multiple reliable witnesses, radar confirmation, and physical evidence that withstands rigorous scrutiny.

In China in the 1970s, for example, Dr. Zha Leping from the Astrophysics Department of Wuhan University and researcher Lin Hongjing investigated a large number of UAP cases. After carefully considering known phenomena, such as strange weather, meteorites, high-altitude balloons, ball lightning, and even earthquake precursor lights, they found many cases that exhibited what Luis Elizondo would later call the "Five Observables." Several events were corroborated by thousands of witnesses, including scientists, pilots, teachers, and military personnel.

One such incident is a 1978 encounter. It concerns an enormous, cigar-shaped object that "carried two bright lights in front and at the tail, and flew from east to west," that was sighted by air force pilots and ground support personnel over Gansu airfield. The object was estimated to be over 1000 meters in length, far beyond the dimensions of any known aircraft, and covered half the sky according to witnesses.

What makes this case particularly intriguing is that the witnesses were watching an outdoor movie at the airfield when the object appeared. This unexpected relationship between outdoor movie-watching and UFO encounters has been documented in the United States as well, most comprehensively in Preston Dennett's *UFOs at the Drive-In: 100 True Cases of Close Encounters at Drive-In Theaters.*

A striking American counterpart to the Gansu airfield account, for example, occurred in August 1974 at the Ascot Auto Theater in Cuyahoga Falls, Ohio. According to witness Scott Santa, then a college student and now a retired Coast Guard radioman with twenty years of service (many involving top-secret clearance as a cryptographer), a whole crowd of theatergoers observed a silent craft moving slowly overhead. The object was massive. It spanned an estimated 274–366 meters from wingtip to wingtip, dwarfing the drive-in by three to four football fields. As it passed overhead, all electricity at the venue failed simultaneously: the movie projector, concession stand lights, and even vehicle engines. Santa further reported that the air became "very heavy," with a visible shimmer "like you see on top of asphalt or cement on a hot day" (Sprague 2021).

What does one do with two such similar cases? Zha and Lin modestly propose in regard to UAP reports in general, "We must adopt an objective attitude of respect for facts [. . .] without brushing aside the possibility of phenomena not yet known." This open-minded, yet curious and searching attitude leaves the door open to multiple hypotheses for the similarities here. Are non-human intelligences drawn to study humans in group entertainment settings? Is there something about the semi-hypnotic state we enter when watching a movie, especially if that meditative state is shared with a large group, that calls or manifests a UAP? Might the shared altered consciousness somehow result in mass hallucination? Or could these "otherworldly" experiences be controlled experiments testing mass reaction and memory suppression on crowds by some unknown human organization?

This cinema-UAP connection also interestingly resonates with Jacques Vallée's cinematic updating of Plato's Allegory of the Cave in his 1990 *Confrontations* (also explored in our Rabbit Hole 19). He argues that UFO encounters might best be thought of as a theatrical performance and critiques those who take them too literally:

"The ufologists behave like social researchers who, trying to understand the phenomena of the cinema, would randomly interview people coming out of the theaters and take their testimony at face value; like the UFO witnesses, these people are not lying. Some of them have seen *Godzilla*, others have seen *Bambi*. The experience, in every case, was real to them. But the reality we should inquire about, the reality UFO researchers are often ignoring, is the movie projector high up in a small, dark, locked room near the ceiling. In that room is the technology that will give you both *Bambi* and *Godzilla*, *Star Wars* and, yes, even *Close Encounters*" (19).

We would add here too that the real intellectual excitement lies not just in realizing UFO experiences might be projected phenomena—but in recognizing that our everyday perception of reality is itself a projection mediated through our senses, and that there is a whole world outside the theater to be explored.

9. IT WAS A DARK AND STORMY NIGHT: WEATHER AND THE ANOMALOUS

In horror movies like Stephen King's *Storm of the Century*, there's often a strong link between severe weather and eruptions of the paranormal. While this might seem like classic literary expressionism, electrical storms do in fact correlate with the paranormal, including UAPs.

Not only that but the electrical connection extends well beyond weather to include car engines dying, streetlights flickering or failing, electronic devices malfunctioning, and witnesses reporting everything from buzzing sounds and tingling sensations to hair standing on end.

Neuroscientist Dr. Michael Persinger is among those who have investigated this connection. He found that paranormal reports do indeed increase during electrical storms. In his 1977 *Space-Time Transients and Unusual Events*, Persinger and researcher Ghislaine Lafrenière proposed a mechanism for why. Electromagnetic fields from tectonic strain stimulate temporal lobe neurons, which create experiences that vary by cultural framework.

This temporal lobe stimulation may explain why the same

atmospheric conditions can trigger various perceptions ranging from UFOs to ghostly apparitions. The experiencers' brains essentially "dial into channel weird"—whether their experiences are then interpreted as brain-based hallucinations or evidence of a sixth sense.

Dr. Harley Rutledge, a physics professor at Southeast Missouri State University, methodically measured this connection. His team recorded significant variations in magnetic field strength and unusual patterns of RF energy during stormy conditions. Similar patterns have been observed in haunting cases, with Dr. William G. Roll, parapsychologist at the University of West Georgia, finding correlations between electromagnetic anomalies and poltergeist episodes.

Such lines of research also potentially explain why some people are sensitive to these experiences. Research by investigator Albert Budden suggests that electromagnetic hypersensitivity is the key factor in differentiating those who experience extraordinary encounters from those who don't when exposed to the same electromagnetic environment. This explains why only certain individuals report paranormal experiences during storms and why some families seem particularly prone to such encounters—reflected in the West by the concept of being born with a "sixth sense," in the East by the belief that some people are born with "yin-yang eyes." It also evokes an interesting link to current conversations about neurodiversity.

Dr. Barry Taff's decades of poltergeist research at UCLA supports this sensitivity theory. Through extensive fieldwork, Taff observed what he calls a consistent "formula" for poltergeist manifestations: locations with geomagnetic anomalies, electromagnetically sensitive individuals with poor coping mechanisms for stress, and certain neurological predispositions such as being seizure-prone or epileptic. Taff found that when these elements combine, the result is often dramatic paranormal activity. "The faces and places may change," Taff explains in a 2020 podcast interview with Jeffrey Mishlove, "but the phenomena do not—the linkage to the central nervous system and hypersensitivity to electromagnetic and geomagnetic fields." Taff's work provides additional evidence for the electromagnetic sensitivity theory, while also highlighting how specific locations become hotspots for such phenomena.

No matter what one makes of the link between storms and anomalous experiences, Chinese cases provide equally strong evidence. We see this in the ancient accounts "The Wheel," "Ships like Shells," and "The Bird with Wheel-Like Wings II." And we see it in contemporary Chinese cases as well.

For instance, in the famous 1994 Meng Zhaoguo incident in Heilongjiang Province, involving a forestry worker who claimed an encounter with, and abduction by, a UFO, investigators recorded anomalous weather patterns. Regional accounts and meteorological reports showed unseasonal snowfall and freezing temperatures in June following the initial UFO sighting, which brings to mind the "cold spots" frequently reported during paranormal encounters.

Multiple witnesses, including loggers and local residents, also reported seeing a massive tornado covering half of Phoenix Mountain, where the encounter took place. They described the tornado as strangely shaped—narrow at the top, bulging at the bottom, with flashing red and blue lights visible within the funnel.

Another fascinating aspect of this case is that after Meng's reported encounter he developed an intense aversion to metal objects, a condition that echoes both Eastern and Western folklore about supernatural entities being "allergic" to iron. Witnesses confirmed that he would fight with his fellow villagers to get any iron away from him. This included a confrontation with a doctor over a stethoscope. Zhang Jingping, an investigator for the World Chinese UFO Association, documented Meng's metallophobia and electrical conductivity anomalies at the alleged landing site.

The storm-anomaly connection also intersects with recent whistleblower testimony, such as that by former NASA chief flight surgeon Dr. Gregory Rogers, who reported witnessing electromagnetic discharges across the surface of a reverse-engineered craft during testing. It aligns as well with the nuclear-UAP relationship explored in Rabbit Hole 10. Nuclear facilities generate distinctive electromagnetic fields, which may attract the same phenomena associated with electrical storms. This could explain why both nuclear sites and storm systems seem to function as attractors for anomalous phenomena. They potentially create similar environmental conditions that either draw these phenomena or make them more perceptible to human observers.

Collectively, these accounts, both ancient and modern, point to a strong cross-cultural link between unexplained phenomena and atmospheric and electromagnetic conditions, though the precise nature of this relationship remains up in the air—so to speak.

10. ATOMIC SPECIAL ATTRACTIONS: UAP INTERACTIONS WITH NUCLEAR FACILITIES

Whatever UFOs are, they have a serious thing for nukes. International Police Service investigator Syed Abdul Kader recently observed unidentified objects hovering over India's Kudankulam Nuclear Power Plant. According to UFO researcher Sabir Hussain, such sightings are part of a broader pattern near nuclear sites throughout India.

This affinity extends far beyond India. In the United States, declassified government files and testimony from military personnel with the highest clearances point to the same connection. Robert Hastings includes such testimony in *UFO and Nukes: Extraordinary Encounters at Nuclear Weapons Sites* via interviews with more than 160 witnesses. Hastings' research shows this connection precedes even the Trinity test in New Mexico, the world's first nuclear explosion on July 16, 1945, long before the advent of drone technology or even the coining of the word "UFO."

In January 1945, for example, luminous balls of light hovered over the Hanford plutonium production site in Washington state. The military scrambled jets to intercept them. But these objects—described by U.S. Navy Lieutenant Clarence "Bud" Clem, who served as a fighter pilot during World War II—easily outmaneuvered the best aircraft. Clem's testimony is backed by declassified Air Force documents. They confirm that "unidentified aircraft" flew over the top-secret Hanford facility on multiple nights that month. Even Roswell itself has a nuclear connection. It housed America's only nuclear bomber squadron, the same unit that dropped bombs on Hiroshima and Nagasaki.

UFOs over nuclear facilities are enough in and of themselves to make anybody lose sleep. But some incidents also involve UFOs directly interfering with U.S. nuclear missile systems.

At Malmstrom Air Force Base in Montana during March 1967, First Lieutenant Robert Salas was on duty one night when his security team reported strange lights making impossible maneuvers in the sky. Minutes later, the same team called back, this time panicking about a red glowing object hovering above the front gate. Then the last thing you want to happen under your watch took place. All ten missiles under Salas's command suddenly went into "no-go condition." They were completely disabled. Ten nuclear-tipped ICBMs rendered useless in seconds. While there were recent attempts to debunk this case, they ironically have strengthened the original testimony. A 2025 *Wall Street Journal* article, for example, claimed electromagnetic pulse testing explained the shutdown, but the documents the article cited showed that EMP testing at Malmstrom didn't begin until 1971—four years after the event witnessed by Captain Salas.

An almost identical incident occurred in 1966 at Minot Air Force Base in North Dakota. Captain David Schindele, a Minuteman I missile launch crew commander, arrived at his post to discover that all ten missiles under his control had gone "off alert" and become unlaunchable. At this same time, security personnel reported a large object, approximately 80–100 feet wide with bright flashing lights, hovering near the facility's perimeter fence.

The Soviet Union has experienced similar incursions. In the early 1990s, investigative journalist George Knapp traveled to Moscow where he conducted extensive interviews with Colonel Boris Sokolov, who had directed the Soviet Ministry of Defense's decade-long UFO research program.

Sokolov revealed that a large disc-shaped and strangely silent object once hovered over a missile base in Soviet Ukraine on October 4, 1982. The object's presence caused missiles to enter countdown mode for 15 seconds before mysteriously shutting down without human intervention.

As Knapp alarmingly put it in testimony for the U.S. House Oversight Committee's July 26, 2023 hearing on Unidentified Anomalous Phenomena: "UFOs appeared over the base, performed astonishing maneuvers in front of stunned eyewitnesses and then somehow took control of the launch system. The missiles were aimed at the US and were suddenly fired up. Launch control codes were somehow entered, and the base was unable to stop what could have initiated World War 3. Then, just as suddenly, the UFOs disappeared, and the launch-control system shut down."

This case mirrors the American incidents, suggesting whatever intelligence is behind these phenomena operates without regard for Cold War boundaries.

Then there's the famous Rendlesham Forest incident of December 1980, often referred to as "Britain's Roswell." This happened near RAF Bentwaters, which housed tactical nuclear weapons. Lieutenant Colonel Charles Halt reported the incident in an official memo to the UK Ministry of Defence. Witnesses reported seeing an object hovering directly over the weapons storage area, sending beams of light downward.

The global pattern of UAP interest in nuclear assets has

continued into the 21st century, documented by official and unofficial sources—in both the West and the East, and on land and at sea.

In 2004, the nuclear carrier USS Nimitz became the site of one of the most documented UAP encounters when Navy pilots tracked a "Tic Tac"-shaped object off California's coast. The encounter was corroborated by radar, infrared video footage, and multiple eyewitnesses. The Department of Defense later declassified and confirmed the videos' authenticity, with similar encounters occurring aboard the USS Theodore Roosevelt from 2014 to 2015, captured in the Pentagon's "Gimbal" and "GoFast" videos.

In Japan, following the 2011 Fukushima Daiichi nuclear disaster, reports of unusual aerial phenomena surfaced in the affected region. Among the many witnesses, Chief Monk Tomonori Izumi of Enmyoin Temple, located near the disaster site, described seeing multiple unidentified flying objects in the aftermath of the explosion. As reported in the Netflix series *Encounters* and by *Vice* magazine, Izumi stated, "The UFOs came after the explosion. There were so many of them. I was shocked." He speculates that the objects might have been attempting to "readjust the flood of radioactive energy."

Russian sources have also reported dramatic incidents involving nuclear submarines and unidentified submerged objects (USOs). According to declassified Russian naval records and testimony from retired Rear Admiral Yury Beketov, a Soviet nuclear submarine during the Cold War detected six unidentified underwater objects traveling at speeds up to 230 knots, far beyond the capabilities of any known submarine. The objects reportedly mirrored the submarine's maneuvers, surfaced alongside it, and then exited the water into the air.

Given the strongly established and unsettling correlation between UAPs and nuclear assets, something strange is clearly going on, and several theories have emerged as to exactly what.

The "benevolent monitoring" hypothesis proposes that non-human intelligences are attempting to prevent human self-destruction. The ability to disable (or in some cases, temporarily activate) nuclear weapons systems could be interpreted as a demonstration or warning about the dangers of these technologies. The "scientific interest" theory, advanced by scientists such as the nuclear physicist Stanton Friedman, suggests that the electromagnetic properties of nuclear reactions might attract UAPs for research or energy purposes. More concerning is the "strategic assessment" theory. It views these incursions as reconnaissance missions by an unknown intelligence (human or non-human) evaluating Earth's defense capabilities. The most speculative theory of all (and perhaps the most fun) involves time travel. It proposes that these phenomena represent future humans monitoring critical junctures in our technological development.

Whatever the truth, this nuclear-UAP connection, wild as it is, represents the most well-documented and consistent pattern in UAP research and shows how high the stakes are for this conversation.

11. WHITE SPACE: MANGA, MANHUA, AND ANOMALOUS ENCOUNTERS

While Japanese manga like Hideshi Hino's or Junji Ito's work might seem like modern innovations, they belong to a long Asian tradition where paintings often include poetic, narrative text that details the underlying scene and story. You can see this, for example, in the ghost scrolls of Luo Ping, an 18th-century Chinese artist. In paintings like his "Ghost Amusement," stretched and distorted figures move through shadowy backgrounds, with narrative text woven among the action, creating a tableau similar to panels in both Hino's and Ito's work.

This image-text intermingling, deeply rooted in the East Asian high art traditions of classical painting, literature, and calligraphy, differs fundamentally from Western comic traditions, which evolved primarily from popular culture forms like political cartoons and newspaper strips.

In other words, while American comics developed out of satirical and serialized storytelling—eventually giving rise to the superhero genre, which is often heavily inflected by political themes, Asian comics inherited other characteristics. Their techniques draw from scroll paintings, ukiyo-e prints, and illustrated texts, emphasizing fluid composition and expressive linework. And their stories are more indebted to philosophy, poetry, myth, and shamanism.

The result is a visual language that treats space differently: using expansive "breath panels" with no dialogue to create mood, employing varied panel sizes that stretch and compress time, and relying on intricate background details that blur the line between environment and emotion. Compare the dense action of a single X-Men page to the contemplative nature shots in a manga like *Mushishi* or Junji Ito's strategic use of white space.

Junji Ito's horror manga *Uzumaki*, about a town haunted by the shape of a spiral, is a great example here too. Despite its spiral obsession evoking the giant spiral UAPs reported across Asia during the time it was written, its detailed linework echoes the meticulous brushwork of traditional ink paintings. Ito's use of negative space and vast, quiet landscapes with little dialogue creates mounting dread in the key of the sublime. This is something one finds as well in classical Asian landscape paintings.

Yuki Urushibara's *Mushishi* also illustrates these characteristics in action. This manga explores the ecological balance between humans and "mushi," primitive lifeforms more fundamental than animals, plants, fungi, or bacteria. These beings predate the divide between material and spiritual reality while embodying elements of both. Sometimes they appear as flying ideograms, other times as something akin to plankton or corn mold, and yet others like shrouded extraterrestrial beings (e.g. "The Green Seat"). The series' sprawling nature scenes and contemplative silent panels evoke traditional Chinese landscape paintings and Japanese woodblock prints. And Urushibara's delicate linework, in tandem with her use of white space and tiny human figures dwarfed by vast landscapes, create a dreamlike quality that underscores themes of interconnectedness in nature and impermanence.

Such techniques enable manga and manhua to seriously explore metaphysics, anomalous phenomena, and shamanism, topics much less frequently explored in Western comics (though Jeffrey Kripal's *Mutants, Mystics, and Superheroes* does a brilliant job of exploring the exceptions). And they create illustrative spaces where pictorial imagination can extend beyond everyday human perception, making visible what might otherwise remain unseen.

This explains why, in Asia, manga and manhua are read extensively by adults and considered major literature, rather than being considered the province of children and socially awkward adults, as in America. In fact, it's pretty common to come across popular Asian dramas, like Korea's *Today's Webtoon* or *W: Two Worlds*, that focus on the lives of webtoon artists, while successful educated adults routinely appear reading webtoons as respectable intellectual engagement even in unrelated dramas.

This cultural sophistication about visual storytelling creates space for exploring extraordinary experiences, including UAPs. In fact, a fascinating UAP account appears in one of the autobiographical interludes Yuki Urushibara placed between episodes of *Mushishi*. In these personal reflections, Urushibara shows how traditional Japanese folklore and family anecdotes about strange phenomena inspired her manga. In one particularly striking account, she shares her grandmother's experience from 1935. Walking along a riverbank at dusk, her grandmother saw "a white moon-like object that did not shine like the moon, slowly floating in the middle of the mountains"—notably not positioned where the moon would be. When her child companion failed to see the object, a local hermit explained it was a "fox trick," reflecting traditional Japanese folklore about kitsune (fox spirits) that were said to travel along that particular path, creating an intriguing link between fox spirit and UAP lore.

What makes this account especially remarkable is how it parallels experiences reported by contemporary Western figures, including President Jimmy Carter. In 1969, while preparing to give a speech in Leary, Georgia, Carter observed a bright object that he compared to the moon. The object changed colors and hovered before moving across the sky in ways no celestial body could. Carter remained cautious about interpreting the sighting, but as president he expressed interest in greater government transparency regarding UFO phenomena. One of his first acts after taking office in 1977 was to make a formal appeal to NASA, requesting that the agency investigate UFO phenomena.

Retired CIA officer John Ramirez provides another strong example. As a boy, Ramirez saw a smooth, moon-like, silver-colored object that descended and then started to float away. And just like Urushibara's grandmother, when Ramirez directed his friends' and cousins' eyes toward it, "they couldn't see anything that I saw. They saw nothing there. Yet I saw it plainly with my eyes."

While no one has committed examples like Ramirez's or Carter's to a graphic art form (as far as we know), comics would be an ideal medium. Out of all the narrative genres, the comic book form stands out as uniquely suited for questioning ordinary assumptions about what's real and possible. As literary theorists like Rosemary Jackson and Kathryn Hume have argued, the "fantastic" is defined by its ability to depart from, and thus challenge or complicate, default notions of consensus reality. Comic art, especially when it breaks from photographic realism, offers just such a departure.

12. SKEPTICISM AND GASLIGHTING

We moderns sometimes act as if skepticism is something we just recently invented, while our feckless ancestors compulsively confabulated crazy things at the slightest provocation: from lands of one-legged cyclopes to forests full of evil, hyper-intelligent chickens (e.g. the dreaded *el pollo maligno*). It's true that every age has its outlandish beliefs and practices, but here's the thing. There's no way we would have survived, let alone thrived, as a species if we were so devoid of critical abilities. After all, reality has a stubborn habit of talking back.

History in fact is riddled with thoughtful doubters. Democritus slept in tombs to disprove the existence of ghosts. Confucius taught his followers to focus on daily life and improving society, rather than on the supernatural, famously advising: "Why worry about serving spirits, until you have learned to serve your fellow people?"—a forerunner of today's popular argument that one should focus on social issues rather than the metaphysical.

Even among cultures that acknowledged the paranormal, they often did so in nuanced, critical ways for which we don't give them credit. Chinese healers carefully distinguished between genuine spirit encounters and psychosomatic maladies caused by improper meditation ("zouhuorumo"). Tibetan medical texts catalogued "sems nad" (illness of the mind) apart from "smyo nad" (madness caused by spirits).

Such cases show that earlier thinkers did not blindly default to otherworldly explanations for phenomena, and at times even showed themselves to be more genuinely open-minded than ourselves and thus less likely to fall into the either/or trap that British writer Colin Wilson described—where there always seems to be enough evidence for the believer, but never enough for the skeptic.

One can still find open-minded approaches today of course, especially among leading intellectuals. A third to half of scientists hold spiritual or supernatural beliefs according to periodic surveys, and there are university initiatives that actively investigate subjects that many people refuse to entertain, such as the University of Virginia's Division of Perceptual Studies, which investigates reincarnation and near-death experiences. Even Albert Einstein wrote an open-minded introduction for Upton Sinclair's book on telepathy, *Mental Radio*. And Alan Turing, the father of computer science and the Turing test, investigated ESP and concluded to his satisfaction that it was scientifically demonstrated.

So why, despite this history of open-minded inquiry, do so many of us react with skepticism to extraordinary experiences, even when compelling evidence and credible witnesses exist?

Some argue this is simply because there are so many hoaxes and frauds associated with this domain. Those certainly exist. But they also exist in nearly every area of human life, from romance to business and politics. Even in the discipline of science, which has probably contributed more to the welfare of human beings than anything else, they exist in large numbers.

Richard Horton, editor of the esteemed medical journal *The Lancet*, suggested in 2015 that potentially half of all scientific research may be false. And the 2021 Dutch National Survey on Research Integrity found that more than half of Dutch scientists regularly engaged in questionable research practices, such as hiding flaws in their research design or selectively citing literature.

So, if the presence of fraud in a field doesn't automatically discount the field (nor should it), we must cast our net wider. When we do, we find one barrier to engaging with the anomalous is our psychological need for ontological stability. By nature, we resist anything that makes the world seem unpredictable. This not only makes us feel safe but also enables the brain to operate with maximum efficiency to conserve energy. Thus, we proclaim to each new lover that our relationship will last forever, convince ourselves that our choices are conscious and logical while ignoring the neurological factors that compromise free will. We blithely go about our days, intentionally forgetting that we're hurtling through space on a rock spinning at over a thousand miles per hour, with a molten core of superheated metals churning beneath our feet—separated from the killing vacuum of space by a paper-thin atmosphere. We avoid thinking about the intestines and gushy parts inside our friends, what's really in a hotdog, or what percentage of insect fragments and rodent hairs the FDA allows in our food.

Research psychologists Thomas Rabeyron and Tianna Loose note that when confronted with anomalous experiences, most people instinctively try to fit them into their existing worldview, rather than adapt their beliefs. This struggle to process the extraordinary leads to significant psychological distress. As they explain it, accepting the extraordinary nature of these experiences is often very difficult, as if a foreign body has entered the psyche, which is then very difficult to integrate.

Think about how strongly people react to others' dietary choices, from recoiling at the thought of eating insects or pig's feet to bristling at someone being vegan. Now multiply that resistance by orders of magnitude when it comes to experiences that challenge our fundamental understanding of reality.

Just as significant though is the high social cost of appearing credulous. Society over-rewards skepticism and over-punishes those who deviate from the status quo. If you doubt a wild claim, you might miss something cool but rarely face serious social consequences. If you believe a false extraordinary claim, however, you risk ridicule, diminished status, and exclusion from faculty parties and family barbecues.

This fear determines what people are willing to say out loud or even to allow themselves to think about. The reluctance to share unusual experiences often stems from the fear of being considered weird or crazy by relatives or medical staff. In a different context but quite similarly, Professors Jeffrey Kripal, Diana Walsh Pasulka, and Gary Nolan have observed that academics routinely conceal their interest in the paranormal out of concern for professional consequences. A 2023 survey found that nearly one in five academics, or their close friends or family, had witnessed something anomalous. Yet many refrained from sharing these experiences, fearing ridicule or professional harm. This is a concern our colleagues and students frequently report as well.

This fear is even more pronounced among pilots and military personnel. Commander David Fravor, whose 2004 Navy encounter with a UAP (the "Tic Tac" incident) was later acknowledged by the Pentagon, has described how military pilots often avoid reporting unusual aerial phenomena for fear of being labeled unstable, grounds for immediate dismissal. In online forums too, civilians frequently express hiding such experiences for decades, citing fear of social and professional repercussions.

The social stigma attached to discussing anomalous experiences cuts across all categories. Whether one is describing a mystical experience of oneness with the universe or talking with a deity, the sense of having psychically perceived information at a distance, or a UAP encounter, the fear of judgment and of being labeled delusional or unstable remains.

This is deeply problematic. Globally, millions of people have reported UFO sightings since the mid-century, five to six percent of these experiencers have reported abductions, and a massive number have had other anomalous experiences. Many of these are extremely traumatic. Given our widespread cultural emphasis on not gaslighting the trauma of others, it is hard to imagine any narrative involving trauma, abduction, and a whole host of non-consensual procedures being so casually or blithely ignored, especially when the experiences sometimes involve children.

This isn't to suggest we should abandon skepticism, but it is to argue that we should apply it, and critical thinking in general, in every direction, including toward our own resistance to the extraordinary. Recognizing the psychological and social factors that shape our resistance to extraordinary experiences helps us do this, as does ontological humility before a reality that consistently proves stranger than our theories about it.

13. COSMIC EGGS

Over the past several decades, an estimated 50-75 high-ranking government, military, and intelligence officials worldwide have risked their careers to publicly discuss encounters with UFOs. France's 1999 COMETA Report, for example, authored by retired generals and defense officials, concluded that a nonhuman intelligence was the most logical explanation for a stubborn core of cases.

This testimony even includes that of not one but *several* national defense ministers. Former Canadian Defence Minister Paul Hellyer (1963–1967) stated unequivocally in 2005 that "UFOs are as real as the airplanes flying overhead" and later claimed that various species of extraterrestrials have been visiting Earth for thousands of years. Former Japanese Defense Minister Shigeru Ishiba acknowledged in 2007 the need for Japan's Self-Defense Forces to develop protocols for UAP encounters, stating that "there are no grounds for us to deny that there are unidentified flying objects and some lifeforms that control them." And in 2020, Haim Eshed, Israel's former Defense Ministry space director, claimed contacts had been made with a "Galactic Federation," composed of several different types of non-human intelligences. With such high-status officials, representing multiple nations across the twentieth and twenty-first centuries, it becomes increasingly difficult to write them all off as cranks or eccentrics—or as participants in a single, unified "Western psy-op," a dismissal that itself begins to look ethnocentric.

Among the most extraordinary testimonies is that of Kirsan Ilyumzhinov, who served simultaneously as president of the Buddhist Republic of Kalmykia from 1993 to 2010 and president of the World Chess Federation (FIDE) from 1995 to 2018. While in office, Ilyumzhinov publicly described being taken aboard an extraterrestrial spacecraft from his Moscow apartment in 1997—an experience he said was corroborated by staff members who could not find him for a period of time before he reappeared in a bedroom they had already searched. The beings wore yellow garments and communicated telepathically, warning that humanity was endangering itself through war, environmental destruction, and an obsession with weapons over genuine progress. He has even speculated that chess—with its 64 black-and-white squares mirroring the 64 codons of the genetic code—was given to humanity by extraterrestrials as a tool for developing consciousness, a kind of yin-yang grid of encoded opposites laid out on a board.

Such individuals keep coming forward, as seen in the 2025 documentary *The Age of Disclosure*, which features interviews with 34 witnesses, including senators and intelligence officers, who alleged long-running secret programs to study and retrieve anomalous craft.

Joining these whistleblowers in January 2025 was U.S. Air Force special ops veteran Jake Barber. In an interview with journalist Ross Coulthart, Barber described recovering what he called an "extraordinary and anomalous" object—about the size of an SUV and shaped like a white, metallic egg, with no engine, no thermal signature, and no visible means of propulsion. Several other military whistleblowers independently supported key elements of Barber's story shortly after his testimony.

This case is compelling enough on its own, regardless of what one makes of it. But what makes it even more compelling is how Barber's description of an egg-shaped craft dovetails with other reports—decades apart in origin, but similar in detail.

One is an account relayed by Eric Taber, a defense aerospace contractor with security clearances and extensive military aircraft experience. In a 2023 interview with *The Daily Mail*'s Josh Boswell, Taber shared a story passed down from his late great uncle, Sam Urquhart, a 28-year Air Force veteran who worked at Area 51 from 1997 to 2014.

According to Taber, Urquhart described a craft that CIA personnel brought to the base in the 1980s for analysis. The object, he said, was egg-shaped, also SUV-sized, and "smooth and seamless," with a silvery-gray, metallic appearance. It lacked control surfaces, exhaust ports, inlets, markings, any visible technology consistent with human engineering.

Engineers at the base reportedly encountered significant difficulties while attempting to study the object. X-rays couldn't penetrate its hull. Physical force had no effect. Its power source and activation method remained completely unknown. In May 2023, Taber provided formal testimony about the account to AARO (the All-domain Anomaly Resolution Office) as part of the Pentagon's broader effort to collect reports related to alleged government possession of non-human craft.

The resemblances between Barber's and Urquhart's accounts are hard to ignore. Both describe egg-shaped objects, metallic and seamless, lacking engines or control systems. Both are about the size of an SUV. Both appear to defy conventional understanding of aerospace engineering. As UFO researcher

Richard Dolan points out in his YouTube podcast episode "Egg Shaped UAP: What You Need to Know," the egg shape has appeared consistently in credible UFO reports for decades, suggesting a specific type of craft with remarkably consistent characteristics: often silent, capable of hovering and extreme acceleration, and frequently described as metallic or shiny in appearance.

Such similarities provoke fascinating questions. For example, these gleaming, egg-shaped, engine-less craft, floating just outside the boundaries of belief, recalls the ancient motif of the cosmic egg, and too Carl Jung's discussion of cosmic egg imagery as a powerful archetype of origin and wholeness, a "mysterious center" of unconscious energies and world creation.

Across multiple cultures, the cosmic egg shows up as a symbol of origin: a sealed, self-contained form out of which the world, time, or even the gods themselves emerge. In Hindu cosmology, such an egg is referred to as the "Hiranyagarbha," the golden womb or egg from which the universe emerged. In ancient Hindu texts like the Vedas (1500–500 BCE), Brahman first creates primordial waters, deposits his seed within them which forms into a cosmic egg, and then gives birth to himself from this egg before creating the rest of the world through thought-acts or the utterance of a primal sound.

In Orphic myth, Phanes, the first god, is born from a radiant silver egg laid by the ebony-winged goddess Nyx in the depths of Erebos. In early Chinese cosmology, Pangu hatches from a primordial egg after 18,000 years, with his breath becoming the wind, his voice the thunder, his body separating to form mountains, rivers, and the earth itself. And on a lighter and more modern note, Mork from Ork in the 1980s sci-fi comedy series *Mork & Mindy* arrives on Earth in a silver egg-shaped spaceship and later lays an egg to "give birth" to his child, Mearth, who refers to Mork as his "mommy."

This sitcom clearly calls back to the "cosmic egg" trope of Jung's. So too, more incredibly, does Barber's case. He describes experiencing what he called "a loving divine feminine connection" in relation to the egg-shaped craft he recovered, an entity he felt continued to guide well after his experience. While certainly odd, this is not a one-off. Contactees routinely describe experiencing a sense of nurturing female beings, protective feminine presences, or craft themselves emanating what witnesses characterize as unmistakably feminine energy. This appears throughout contemporary accounts, from that of Whitley Streiber to that of Chris Bledsoe, as well as ancient accounts discussed elsewhere in this book.

None of this is to say that Barber or Taber stumbled into a myth. But when contemporary, high-credibility accounts start describing radiant, seamless eggs appearing in the margins of classified aerospace programs, ones moreover associated with feminine energy, it's hard not to feel the tug of archetypes in your gut. And one has to consider these stories don't just suggest something new happening in the world. They suggest too that something very old masked by ancient mythologies might still be happening, pressing through into the present and interpreted into new forms.

14. THE SHAPES OF THINGS: UAP TRANSFORMATIONS IN EASTERN AND WESTERN ACCOUNTS

One expects aircraft to come in a few basic shapes, in line with physics and mimicking birds or bugs. Even if they get more exotic, as some satellites and experimental aircraft do, we still expect them to maintain consistent shapes and sizes during encounters. But one of the most unsettling aspects of UAP reports is how often witnesses describe objects that morph, merge, split, or radically change size mid-encounter, defying our basic assumptions about how physical objects behave.

In a 1980 survey, Chinese researchers Dr. Zha Leping and Lin Hongjing found that Chinese unidentified flying objects occurred mainly in three distinct categories of shapes. The first category included disk or globe-shaped craft (including oval and egg variants). These account for approximately 80% of all sightings, typically appearing silver in daylight while emitting orange-red light at night.

The remaining sightings were split between extraordinarily large, elongated objects sometimes exceeding 1,000 meters in length, and spiral, *Uzumaki*-shaped phenomena with bright central cores and radiating arms of light. This is roughly in line with current Western statistics, although in the West, spiral sightings are not common.

But these neat categories break down when witnesses describe the same object dramatically changing size or shifting between forms during a single encounter, seemingly operating outside the playground rules of spacetime. For instance, in 2017, multiple witnesses in Salento, Italy, observed and recorded a UFO that morphed from a glowing orb to an elongated cigar shape, then into a circular, doughnut-like form (with shifts in color from greenish to white) before reverting to its original form and fading away.

The classical Chinese account "The Top" (1561) provides a historical instance of this: an object with a pointy top and broad base descends slowly while lights pulse from its surface. Then, without warning, it suddenly swells to ten times its original size. Not moving closer to appear larger, but experiencing an actual, inexplicable expansion that witnesses noted could not be attributed to a change in distance.

Multiple UAPs have also been sighted merging into one and, conversely, one UAP has been observed splitting into separate ones. In the Hudson Valley UFO wave of the 1980s, thousands of independent witnesses described a massive, boomerang-shaped craft that sometimes appeared to split into smaller lights, only to re-form moments later.

Even more bizarre are those cases where multiple witnesses perceive the same phenomenon completely differently. In 2012, for example, attorney Rey Hernandez and his wife Dulce simultaneously encountered the same anomalous event yet described entirely different objects. Dulce, with her Catholic background, interpreted what she saw as an "angel" and described a U-shaped object emitting a green scanning light. Rey, an atheist at the time, observed an "energy being" that was rectangular, about 2.5 feet wide by 1 foot tall, made of swirling colors "like paint being stirred," and semi-transparent without hard edges.

The famous October 13, 1917 Fatima incidents in Portugal provide an even more dramatic example. Among an estimated 70,000 witnesses, some reported seeing the sun itself "dancing," changing colors, moving in zigzag patterns across the sky and plummeting toward earth, while others described a silvery disc-like object distinct from the sun that moved in unusual ways. Still others saw the Virgin Mary. According to researchers Joaquim Fernandes and Fina D'Armada, these perceptual variations correlated strongly with witnesses' religious and cultural backgrounds.

Two other details stand out during the Fatima account. Despite heavy rainfall that left everyone soaked and the ground muddy, some witnesses reported their clothes and the ground around them dried instantly after the event, while others described a shower of rose petals in colors never seen before that fell and mysteriously disappeared. Interestingly, never-before-seen colors also appear in other paranormal narratives. This includes both "real-world" clinical reports of near-death experiences and "mythical" folktales of journeys to magical realms such as China's Kunlun where radiant colors shift like the aurora or the Japanese underwater Dragon Palace which is filled with colors that cannot be described upon one's return to the human world.

An event similar to Fatima occurred in Zeitoun, Egypt, as documented by Travis Dumsday, Associate Professor of Philosophy and Religious Studies at Concordia University. Between 1968 and 1971, hundreds of thousands of predominantly Muslim witnesses observed luminous apparitions above St. Mary's Coptic Orthodox Church. Some saw a luminous, three-dimensional and fully formed figure, which appeared sometimes for minutes and other times for hours. These witnesses described the figure as "animate" and "lifelike" with distinct facial features—bowing to the crowd, moving around the dome, and behaving in ways that distinguished it from a static projection. Others described seeing simply "a line of light" that would "grow and expand" into a general luminous form.

Researcher Douglas Scott Rogo suggests in *The Haunted Universe* that such manifestations reflect the ability of the human mind to generate "thought-forms" that can take on objective reality, similar to the concept of "tulpas" in Tibetan mysticism. According to this "internal generation theory," intense collective focus might unconsciously create psychic entities with quasi-independent existence, explaining both the physicality of these phenomena (sometimes captured in photographs) and the perceptual variations among witnesses.

While the ability to dramatically shift structure in such a manner conflicts with our usual understandings of physics and psychology, it is a fascinating feature that repeatedly occurs in UAP and other paranormal accounts across cultures and links directly to global bodies of folklore about shapeshifters. Ultimately, it suggests what has become a major theme across the sections of this book: the existence of a deeper reality where perception and manifestation are interconnected.

15. ASIAN IMMORTALS, FAIRIES, AND OTHER TRICKSTERS OF THE LIGHT

Fairy-like beings haunt the mythologies of every continent, from the Chinese *xian* and the Celtic *sidhe* to the Japanese *kitsune*. That's fascinating enough. But the real kicker is how well these stories collectively map onto contemporary reports of alien encounters—trickster-like entities traversing realms, manipulating time, deploying paranormal powers, and abducting humans.

To fully appreciate these parallels, it's important to understand that before their Victorian transformation into sanitized sprites for children's stories, fairies in the European tradition were powerful, dangerous, human-sized beings. Earlier generations genuinely feared what the Victorians later miniaturized, domesticated, and dressed in funny hats and petal-skirts—a move that children's literature and the toy industry frequently make to defang nightmares.

Angela Bourke's *The Burning of Bridget Cleary* exposes this darker reality through a horrific 1895 case in which a husband killed his wife, believing she had been replaced by a fairy changeling. It was one of many such Irish cases at the time, illustrating what Bourke frames as a collision between traditional belief and modernizing Ireland. Even today, fairy beliefs persist, in countries like Iceland, where surveys consistently show that up to 50% of the population maintains openness to belief in the *huldufólk*, or hidden people. Roads and buildings are rerouted to avoid disturbing "elf" habitats, and encounters are regularly reported.

Those who claim such experiences describe profound psychological effects identical to alien abductees: altered personalities, missing time, unexplained illnesses, acquisition of secret knowledge. They also face similar social responses—mockery and fascination at best, ostracism and persecution at worst.

Asian testimonies show the same patterns. In Ji Yun's 18th-century story "Guests from the Sky" (included in "Sightings"), Shen Tiechan encounters rotating orbs of light in the sky, luminous spheres that evoke both fairy lights and the modern UAP sightings. From these orbs emerge female servants of a xian nü (female Chinese immortal), who teleport Shen against his will to a strange room where their mistress is waiting. Regular meetings with the xian nü dramatically alter his personality and eventually prove fatal. This account, with its aerial phenomena, involuntary transport, and dramatic physical effects, predates modern UFO culture by over 150 years yet bears striking similarity to contemporary alien abduction narratives.

Hidden Realms

The xian nü's non-terrestrial location reveals another crucial overlap. Both classical nonhuman (or superhuman) entities and today's nonhuman intelligences inhabit hidden realms (celestial, subterranean, or dimensional) accessible only through specific portals or other non-traditional means, and existing alongside but separate from the mundane world.

This concept of hidden adjacent realms appears in both Western fairy lore and well-documented UAP phenomena. Pre-Victorian Celtic traditions describe *Tír na nÓg* (Land of Youth), a dimension accessible only through specific portals or during cosmic alignments. Similarly, scientific investigations at Skinwalker Ranch have reported objects transitioning between visibility and invisibility, including a triangular craft emerging from what researchers described as an "opening" in the sky. During the Hudson Valley wave of 1982-1986, thousands saw massive craft materialize overhead, then either accelerate impossibly or simply "blink out" of existence—appearing to phase in and out of reality.

Beyond spatial liminality, manipulation of time is another striking parallel.

In the Han dynasty legend of Liu Chen and Ruan Zhao, two men follow immortal maidens (xian nü) to their realm, experiencing what feels like half a year—only to return home and find centuries had passed. This pattern repeats in the Jin Dynasty story of Wang Zhi, who, while chopping wood on a mountain, encounters immortal children playing chess. He stays for what feels like a single match, but upon arriving home, he finds that generations have elapsed. Both these narratives mirror the missing time of European fairy tales. So too do contemporary UAP cases.

Former Pentagon AATIP director Luis Elizondo documented a pilot's encounter that seemed to last only five minutes, yet whose instruments showed thirty minutes had passed, a discrepancy recorded in official flight logs. And in the 1976 Allagash Waterway incident, four men lost two hours from their awareness, a gap corroborated by polygraph and consistent independent accounts.

Such temporal distortions suggest encounters with entities or places that possess a fundamentally different relationship to spacetime than human beings do. This kind of malleability is not out of the realm of possibility in physics either. As Einstein observed, "Time and space are modes by which we think and not conditions in which we live." His insight resonates powerfully with both ancient fairy lore and modern UAP accounts, where we confront beings who seem to manipulate these "modes of thinking" in ways we cannot, rather than being bound by them. This same alarming freedom is reflected as well in their frequent, and seemingly willful, bizarre behavior and appearances.

Trickster Logic

Fairies behave bizarrely. They laugh at funerals and cry at births. In his 1691 study *The Secret Commonwealth of Elves, Fauns, and Fairies*, Reverend Robert Kirk, an educated minister who took fairies seriously, described them as a "subterranean and (for the most part) invisible people [. . .] of a middle nature betwixt man and angel," with "intelligent studious spirits, and light changeable bodies (like those called astral)." His detailed observations reveal the long history of trickster qualities in these fairy accounts.

This same trickster logic permeates Asian folklore. In zhiguai literature, ancient accounts of anomalies, mountain imps (*shan xiao*) delight in reversing causal relationships, telling lost merchants to "turn back to reach the village ahead." Immortals speak in riddles, as in Wang Guan's Tang dynasty account of the Yellow Emperor meeting an old man who claims to be both a thousand years old and unborn (which is said to be based on earlier anecdotes shared by Ge Hong). Zen Buddhist koans use similar linguistic subversions like "What is the sound of one hand clapping?" These are deliberate contradictions designed to rupture ordinary cognition and push perception beyond dualistic thinking into the terrain of poetic consciousness.

Modern alien encounters feature similar cognitive disruption: human-sized glowing owls and talking raccoons that recall fairy tale animals, miniature or doubled people, and perplexing sexual requests. Jacques Vallée describes several examples in *Passport to Magonia*: aliens who hand out pancakes lacking salt to a bewildered Wisconsin farmer (1961) and UFO entities who claim to hail from places like "anywhere, but we'll be in Greece day after tomorrow" (1897). The "Black Hands" case in France involved a woman approached by two disembodied, black-gloved hands that emerged from a light in the sky. And Men in Black (MIB) encounters feature figures alternately theorized as government agents, aliens in disguise, or interfaces with aspects of reality beyond human comprehension—similar to the role of the agents in *The Matrix*.

In *The Mothman Prophecies*, John Keel documents how MIB display odd social behaviors and speech seemingly designed to destabilize witnesses' reality. In a 1976 case, Dr. Herbert Hopkins, investigating a UAP abduction in Maine, received a phone call requesting an immediate meeting. Minutes later, a man appeared at his door in a perfectly tailored black suit despite no vehicle being seen in the area. The visitor had unnaturally white skin without facial hair—not even eyebrows or eyelashes. Hopkins reported that the MIB spoke in monotone, periodically stopping mid-sentence as if receiving instructions, and commanded Hopkins to watch as he made a coin in his palm turn silvery, then blueish, then disintegrate. Before leaving, the visitor instructed Hopkins to destroy his research materials, stating, "Neither you nor anyone else on this plane will ever see that coin again." Hopkins later discovered a colleague had received an identical visitor that same night.

These linguistically aberrant encounters function as catalysts for cognitive transformation. This brings to mind psychologist Jerome Bruner's observation in *Actual Minds, Possible Worlds* that paradoxical language creates "subjunctivity"—a state of mental receptivity he likened to "the grammar of possibility" that allows alternative realities to take root. As Bruner argues, paradox gives rise to a temporary suspension of our usual meaning-making apparatus, allowing new structures of understanding to emerge.

Similarly, in *Making Sense of Nonsense*, Raymond Moody, trained as both a physician and a philosopher, argues that nonsensical language serves as a "logical bridge" between ordinary rationality and mystical insight. This parallels Zen master Shunryu Suzuki's insistence that reality cannot be caught by thinking or feeling mind and his presentation of paradox as a tool for creating what he calls "beginner's mind"—a state where "there are many possibilities" precisely because conventional thinking has been temporarily suspended.

Cultivation and Contact

Scholars rightly caution against conflating distinct cultural figures like Chinese *xian* with European fairies. The term *xian*, while it often refers to non-human celestial deities or nature spirits in Chinese culture, also specifically designates transcendent immortals who achieved spiritual elevation through self-cultivation, a core concept in Taoist philosophy evident in *xian*'s Chinese character (仙)—showing a human figure beside a mountain, suggesting ascetics who withdrew to sacred peaks to pursue immortality. This distinguishes the *xian* from the more capricious European fairy, whose Latin origins trace back to *fata* —the Fates themselves—beings controlling human destiny.

Certain Celtic traditions do attribute superior spiritual qualities to fairy beings. The Sidhe (*Aos Sí*) were sometimes regarded as "spiritually perfect" beings and venerated as ancestral guardians. However, with the exception of the deeply ecological concern associated with them (also present in xian nü accounts), their concerns are typically depicted as inherent rather than attained through spiritual practice, marking a significant distinction between traditions.

This distinction between inherent and cultivated abilities however blurs significantly when comparing Asian traditions with contemporary UAP encounters in the West. Here, the connection between entities, experiencers, and spiritual cultivation practices becomes unmistakable. According to the *Shenxian zhuan* (*Biographies of Spirit Immortals*, c. 317 CE), there are four distinct schools of immortality cultivation: *qi* (breath control and meditation), *shi* (dietary practices and abstention from certain foods), *fangzhong shu* (sexual yoga), and *dan* (alchemical practices). Each represents a different approach to transcendence, but all require disciplined cultivation rather than innate supernatural abilities.

Such attempts at self-cultivation appear across UAP modern experiences, both in terms of practices undertaken and benefits claimed. Dr. Steven Greer's CE5 protocol explicitly employs meditation techniques to initiate contact with extraterrestrial intelligence, methods recognizable to Taoist practitioners seeking connection with *xian* beings. What experiencers report gaining mirrors such connections: spiritual evolution, consciousness expansion, and a sense of potential transcendence beyond physical limitations. Similarly, The Monroe Institute's Gateway Process, once used by the CIA to train remote viewers, employs breathwork, energy movement practices, and deep meditation to achieve altered states conducive to contact. Throughout the history of UAP contact, as documented in sources like Chris Bledsoe's memoir *UFO of God*, accessing UAP phenomena—whether interpreted as extraterrestrial, supernatural, or psychological—requires similar transformations of consciousness.

This pattern of preparation for contact extends beyond group protocols into individual practices. Dr. Diana Walsh Pasulka's *American Cosmic* features "Tyler D." (widely identified as Timothy Taylor, a NASA engineer) who employs specific physical and mental regimens to prepare for contact with the phenomenon. These protocols emphasize maintaining a "physical and electrical balance" as preparatory measures for engaging with anomalous phenomena—regimens reminiscent of both aspiring *xian* and contemporary pioneers like Jack Parsons, the rocket scientist who, while helping establish what would become NASA's Jet Propulsion Laboratory, simultaneously developed ceremonial practices aimed at establishing contact with non-human intelligences (as further described in Rabbit Hole 16).

These modern approaches, whether group or individual, echo ancient understandings of how humans access extraordinary domains. In Taoist cosmology, perceiving and interacting with *xian* required becoming like them through gradual transformation of one's own consciousness and vital energies. As the 12th century CE *Zhong Lü Chuandao Ji* (*Anthology of the Transmission of the Tao*) explains, the path from human to immortal is marked by the refinement of yin energy into pure yang, resulting in the transcendence of ordinary human limitations. This suggests that contact with otherworldly beings may require a corresponding elevation in the observer's own energetic state—a concept that resonates with modern contact experiences, which repeatedly stress the importance of non-dualistic thinking, the cultivation of love and compassion, and thus the "raising of one's frequency," almost like a child standing on their tippytoes to peer over a fence.

This idea finds support in research from the Dr. Edgar Mitchell Foundation, which surveyed more than 4000 individuals reporting UAP contact experiences. According to the neuroscientist Dr. Robert Davis, who was involved in the study, about 40–50% say they receive spiritual messages, technological information, and guidance about their life.

This convergence suggests that what ancient traditions conceptualized as spiritual cultivation closely corresponds to what contemporary researchers describe as consciousness attunement—both serving as technologies for facilitating contact with intelligences beyond conventional reality.

Bridging the Binary

Numerous other congruences shared between these bodies of lore stand out: the ability of non-human entities to employ fox-trick "glamour," cloud minds, and manipulate perception of their physical appearance or physical reality; their strong association with the souls of the dead; the motif of talking animals; food taboos surrounding offerings from these entities; water as a portal to other worlds; cross-species sexual encounters that yield hybrids; self-presentation as guardians of nature; an ability to travel between after-life and physical-life realms; and the entities' association with mandala-like formations including fairy rings, ritual circles, and crop circles. These themes are insightfully explored by a range of contemporary researchers, from Diana Walsh Pasulka to Joshua Cutchin.

As previously mentioned, researchers warn against framing Asian immortals as "fairy" in ways that erase the unique philosophical and spiritual context of Asian traditions and reduce these traditions to dim reflections of Western culture. Yet one must also avoid adopting a purely Western academic binary, dividing concepts into rigid opposites, while doing comparative work. As the Chinese philosopher Zhuangzi reminds us: "If we insist on seeing things solely in terms of their differences, then even our inner organs are as far apart as the states of Chu and Yue." By recognizing both similarity and difference and embracing Buddhist both/and logic (where something can be true and not true, similar and dissimilar), we adopt the necessary beginner's mind to perceive intersections and patterns.

These cross-cultural patterns—spanning fairy encounters, *xian* traditions, and modern UAP reports—provoke questions that resist easy answers. Are they reflections of universal structures in the human unconscious? Neurological constants generating similar experiences across cultures? Or do they encode realities and entities at the very edge of perception? Whatever explanation one favors, these parallels deserve a second look, and a third too.

16. THAT'S AMORE: A GLOBAL HISTORY OF SEXUAL ENCOUNTERS WITH NON-HUMAN ENTITIES

Amoebas at the start were not complex; They tore themselves apart and started Sex.

—Arthur Guiterman Homage Poem

Sex is the best form of fusion at room temperature.

—Anonymous

Contemporary claims of sexual contact with UAP entities are merely the latest entry in humanity's strange, ongoing sex diary of otherworldly intimacy. Mesopotamian texts dating back millennia describe incubus-like entities slipping into bedrooms at night. Islamic traditions tell of djinn, born from "smokeless fire," who coupled with humans. Greek, Roman, and Hindu myths teem with gods who can't resist mortal warmth. And Indian traditions record cases in which repeated spiritual sexual encounters lead to illness, even death, as a result of apsaras (celestial nymphs) and yakshis (nature spirits) gradually siphoning off a person's prana—their vital life force.

East Asia offers its own accounts. Beyond the famous tales of fox spirits seducing victims (also feared for their ability to drain life energy), Korea preserves substantial shamanic testimonies documenting female shamans (*manshin*) who maintained decades-long relationships with mountain god spirits (*sanshin*). The spirits visited in dreams and sometimes in manifested flesh, leaving visible bite marks. This shamanic tradition appears across Asia, including China, where it is immortalized in the *Nine Songs*, an ancient poetic cycle that chronicles shamanic séances and love affairs with spirits, and in Japan via *yūrei* legends of ghost lovers.

By the early modern period, Western occult literature for its part included instructional texts for initiating encounters with entities ranging from fairies to incubi, as documented in Frank Klaassen and Katrina Bens's 2013 "Achieving Invisibility and Having Sex with Spirits: Six Operations from an English Magic Collection ca. 1600." It included as well witch-hunters' handbooks, which explored demonic intercourse with obsessive precision. The *Malleus Maleficarum* (1487) described in excited detail how female demons, wearing soft but illusory flesh, drained human seed from sleeping men so that male demons could then ejaculate it into human women.

This grotesque cycle of biological piracy, the authors claimed, was a way for the Devil to mock divine creation while also populating the world with corrupted flesh. And it is a clear forerunner to today's conversations about extraterrestrial genetic tampering and claims related to hybrid offspring.

However, not all human-spirit liaisons were regarded as antithetical to Christianity. Christian mystics frequently used erotically charged language themselves to describe encounters with angels and even Jesus himself, such as St. Teresa of Ávila's famous account of an angel plunging his golden spear into her heart repeatedly, leaving her in ecstasy and "aflame with a great love of God."

Modern Spectrophilia and Celebrity Encounters

Such cross-species encounters have shown great staying power. And modern reports of spectrophilia, sexual attraction to or encounters with ghosts or spirits, are remarkably consistent with historical accounts.

This includes intimate encounters described by well-known public figures. Actress Lucy Liu told *Us Weekly* about a sexual encounter with a ghost on her futon. "Some sort of spirit came down from God knows where and made love to me [. . .]. It was sheer bliss. I felt everything. I climaxed. And then he floated away. It was almost like what might have happened to Mary. That's how it felt. Something came down and touched me, and now it watched over me."

Likewise, actress Anna Nicole Smith told *FHM* magazine about repeated encounters with a spectral lover: "A ghost would crawl up my leg and have sex with me at an apartment a long time ago in Texas." She emphasized the consensual nature of these encounters: "He's never hurt me, and he just gave me some amazing sex so I have no problem." Singer Kesha even revealed her song "Supernatural" emerged from "having sexy time with a ghost."

Not all such encounters are welcome. Indeed, like historical cases, several are clearly assault. Model Coco Austin, who is married to the rapper Ice-T, reported a nonconsensual and upsetting encounter with a perverted ghost that physically mauled her clothing. The most extensively documented case, however, involves Doris Bither, investigated in 1974 by UCLA researchers led by Dr. Barry Taff. Bither claimed to be repeatedly raped by a ghost. Researchers initially dismissed her story, but subsequent investigation revealed phenomena that multiple observers, including scientists and professional photographers, witnessed simultaneously. The team documented unusual balls of light moving around her bedroom and captured photographs of arcs of light framing Bither on her bed. At one point, the researchers observed lights coalescing into the partial form of a tall male figure visible from the lower diaphragm upward. This case became the basis for the 1982 film *The Entity*.

UAP Abductions and Sexual Contact

Reports of sexual encounters with non-human intelligences extend beyond ghosts to UAP-related entities. While such experiences are often mocked, as was Bither's case initially, their scope deserves serious consideration, particularly since some occur in full consciousness during the day, making sleep paralysis, the go-to explanation, insufficient for some accounts.

A comprehensive 1992 Roper survey on "unusual personal experiences" estimated that 1–2% of American adults (roughly 3.3 to 3.7 million people) have had experiences identified as, or nearly identical to what's consistently identified as alien abduction. More recently, in 2025, Jim Semivan, a retired CIA Senior Intelligence Service officer, offered a more conservative estimate, suggesting about half a million Americans have had such experiences.

Regardless of whether the higher or lower number is more accurate, they're both large and a notable subset of these individuals report sexual contact during abductions, many traumatic. And if trauma accounts on this scale emerged from any other demographic, sexual or nonsexual, they would draw serious attention, particularly given that many experiencers are otherwise ordinary people, including parents, construction workers, teachers, and pilots, without a history of making fantastic claims or interest in the paranormal.

Dr. Christopher Green, a physician and neuroscientist formerly with the CIA, authored a 2010 Defense Intelligence study on acute and subacute neurological and dermal injuries in people exposed to anomalous aerospace phenomena. His report concluded that many of these cases involved genuine trauma with clear medical and neuropsychiatric effects. Other researchers have reported similarly serious impacts among people describing entity encounters, even though there is disagreement about whether the cause is an actual external event, a psychological "false memory," or a neurological anomaly. Among these researchers are Drs. Richard McNally and Susan Clancy at Harvard, who have documented strong trauma-like physiological responses when self-identified abductees recall their experiences, and Drs. José I. Latorre and María Y. Vellisca, who have described significant post-traumatic and dissociative symptoms in abduction claimants.

Yet many experiencers describe more than trauma. In *Transformation* and subsequent works, abductee Whitley Strieber reflected on his sexual experiences, particularly with one female visitor. He described their encounter as the most intense in his life, yet ultimately not about sexual pleasure or reproduction, the typical goals of sex, but rather a fusion designed for energy exchange and direct interface between two radically different consciousnesses.

The deep intimacy of such contact is interpreted by our brain as sexual, since that's the best "grammar" we have for it. But Strieber suggests it's something beyond this, something that involves overcoming our individual egos and accessing a deeper level of being.

This transcendental interpretation might sound like the racier passages in adult sci-fi, but it evokes ancient spiritual traditions that understood sexuality as one of the most ancient rituals (and a prototype for all others), as well as a primal creative force driving us toward connection with not only other beings but other states of consciousness. And this was a force that could be channeled and directed.

Eastern and Western Erotic Spiritual Practices

The Chinese Taoist tradition, for example, developed sexual practices known as *fangzhong shu* (房中术) or "arts of the bedchamber" as pathways to longevity and spiritual transcendence.

These practices, which flourished between the Han and Tang dynasties (206 BCE to 907 CE), centered on "joining energy"—practitioners harnessing sexuality for spiritual advancement. While male retention of semen in such practices is well known (and still practiced by athletes and occultists world-over), what's less known is that female orgasm was held as equally essential. Women's sexual fulfillment generated additional jing energy that male practitioners sought to absorb and redirect. Thus, the female body was approached with reverence, with the vagina referred to as the "Jade Fountain," female breasts as "Bells of Love," and the clitoris as the "Yin Bean."

Hindu and Buddhist tantric traditions also approached sexuality as a vehicle for spiritual transformation, aiming to channel orgasmic energy upward through chakras, bypassing physical release.

The West evolved its own occult erotic traditions that continue up to the present day. The 19th-century African American occultist Paschal Beverly Randolph developed the first systematic Western teachings on sex magic, viewing orgasm as a portal to divine energy. His practitioners visualized their desired outcome during "nuptive prayer" while maintaining complete verbal silence. And Napoleon Hill, author of the perennial bestseller *Think and Grow Rich*, shared similar views. Religious historian Mitch Horowitz traces how these explicit sexual techniques and their larger philosophies were gradually sanitized for mainstream consumption, evolving into "creative visualization" and "the law of attraction."

Cultural icon Aleister Crowley, whose ideas influenced musicians ranging from Ozzy Osbourne and Iron Maiden to Led Zeppelin, David Bowie, and the Beatles (creating a hidden occult thread in Western popular music), expanded on such concepts. He viewed sexual energy as nature's most primal force, and orgasm as a state of consciousness key to accessing magical power. One of Crowley's most distinctive techniques was "eroto-comatose lucidity," a complex ritual designed to induce altered consciousness through sexual exhaustion. The practice involved multiple attendants whose duty was to repeatedly exhaust and rouse the ritualist sexually until they entered a trance state between sleep and wakefulness.

But perhaps the most compelling example of sex magick is the work of the Aleister Crowley-inspired engineer Jack Parsons (1914–1952). Co-founder of what became NASA's Jet Propulsion Laboratory and pioneer of the solid rocket fuel technology that launched America's space program, Parsons simultaneously practiced elaborate sexual rituals designed to manifest otherworldly entities—work he believed directly benefited his aerospace projects.

This synthesis exemplifies what Dr. Diana Walsh Pasulka describes as a "cosmist tradition," a contemporary spirituality popular among a small set of scientists, that treats advanced technology as sacred and promotes contact with non-human intelligences.

Contemporary Research and Theoretical Frameworks

While the historical occult traditions we've glossed were rooted in centuries-old magical lineages and their associated worldviews, similar conclusions emerge from contemporary experiencers who usually lack training in such practices.

Research from the Foundation for Research into Extraterrestrial and Extraordinary Experiences (FREE) reveals that individuals reporting sexual entity contact frequently describe it not in terms of physical pleasure but as energetic communion, with reported transformative aftereffects that run the gamut from enhanced intuition to psychical abilities that persist long after the encounter.

What sense can one make of this conceptual overlap? If there is a throughline, it may be that, as Dr. Jeffrey Kripal of Rice University theorizes, sexuality can dissolve the boundaries ordinarily drawn between self and other, body and spirit, opening access to broader, even cosmic, states of consciousness.

We don't need occult philosophy to appreciate this point, either. The everyday language of sexuality is rife with allusions centered on a dissolution of boundaries. Not just via the classic "two becoming one" or "the beast with two backs" metaphors, but in how sex is discussed across cultures in terms of consumption ("devouring," "licking," "swallowing whole"), violence ("splitting open"), and transformation ("melting together"), something one finds in religious language as well.

Even in our daily life, sexuality can be said to operate as an advanced interface technology—a joining of biological hardware and psychological software that allows radically different forms of consciousness to connect and exchange information and sensation.

This shamanic ego-busting and transcendent quality explains why diverse traditions, from Taoist bedchamber arts to Western ceremonial magic, have incorporated sexuality into spiritual practice. After all, for most people, orgasm represents a profound and easy-to-access altered state of consciousness that strongly resembles those found in mystical experiences and seizure states. While some experience mechanically rote, pull-and-release pleasure through sex, others (especially women) report entering trance-like states where awareness of time and space fades.

Those with sexual synesthesia describe even more extraordinary experiences—geometric patterns, fireworks, metallic tastes, or glimpses of architecture made of light. Research by clinical psychologist Jacques van Lankveld, former president of the International Academy of Sex Research, confirms that altered states of consciousness are strongly linked to sexual responsiveness, suggesting that the boundaries between mind, body, and sensation naturally blur during sexual experience.

Competing Hypotheses

This consciousness-shifting characteristic is perhaps our favorite theory for why sexuality features so prominently (and weirdly) in accounts of human-UAP entity interaction. That said, there are other popular theories. The energetic feeding hypothesis suggests sexual energy, like intense emotions such as fear, serves as "fuel" for vampiric non-material entities—a concept well known to Goth punks who are largely unaware of the concept's roots in Taoist practice and Jack Parsons' ritual work. Various genetic extraction hypotheses propose that what is perceived as sex might actually be VR-induced hallucination masking genetic sampling performed by extraterrestrials conducting research or time travelers from our species' future, desperately harvesting ancestral DNA to repair their degraded genome.

And one has to be open to the concept of multidimensional,

ultraterrestrial, or interstellar sex tourism as well because why not? We should resist the prudish assumption that a technologically advanced species would be less libidinous than ourselves. After all, the animal kingdom offers a menagerie of cross-species sexual encounters from Japanese macaques attempting to mate with sika deer to what our dogs have tried to do with stuffed animals in the house. Even our own DNA reveals ancient cross-species breeding between Homo sapiens, Neanderthals, and Denisovans. If our ancestors were comfortable enough with other hominid species to produce fertile offspring, why assume advanced beings would find cross-species contact abhorrent?

As for us moderns, despite our Victorian protestations, experimental sexual practices remain the norm rather than exception, from elaborate role-playing to BDSM. Ultimately, all these speculations suggest that sexuality may function as a genuine technology for altering consciousness and facilitating contact with non-ordinary realities, and not just as a cheap way to have fun. And they draw our attention to the hidden depths of our own sexual practices and invite us to recognize that everyday human sexuality can sometimes be a portal to extraordinary states of consciousness.

17. SHAMANS AND ALIENS

My aunt*, a businesswoman in Zibo, has always possessed "the gift," an ability to predict when this or that relative or friend will die. Yet, after she recently began a daily meditation, her gifts hit a whole new level. She can see past lives, converse with the dead, and has access to new sensitivities and forms of knowledge that stun even her.

A few weeks ago, she spoke with a qigong master who asked her if she practiced qigong. She told him, "No." He replied, "Well, you should start, because your sky eye is all the way open now."

Though my aunt is worldly and grounded, fond of red wine and her pet chickens, and would never call herself such, she has become, in essence, a shaman. Indeed, one of the most incredible moments she told me about concerns a visit from my dead grandfather where she became him while he visited, reflecting the shamanic idea that when one truly sees something one

---

* Yi Izzy Yu speaks for the duration of this note.

becomes it. This is a perfect illustration of the Zen saying: "When you see a bluebird, become the bluebird."

The world is full of shamans. Shaman attorneys. Shaman engineers. Shaman IRS agents. A shaman is simply someone who perceives and interacts with spirit worlds, using the knowledge they gain to help our world. While some are born with natural gifts, their abilities often only fully awaken through dramatic events: serious illness, major life transitions, or intentional consciousness-shifting practices like intensive meditation or fasting.

Many scholars consider shamanism the wellspring of all religions, making its perspectives invaluable for examining UAP encounters. These encounters have recently both influenced existing religious traditions and spawned new ones. Too, shamanic traditions are built around the recognition of multiple orders of reality operating simultaneously, with both shamans and UAPs believed to be able to cross dimensional boundaries at will.

Religious studies specialist Peter Levenda is instructive here. During an *Engaging the Phenomenon* podcast centered on UAPs, he notes that indigenous peoples of South America have built-in traditions for interacting with non-human intelligences. These include strategies for productive coexistence and the use of tribal specialists in the science of such realities. "But for us, we've lost that," Levenda observes. "We're going at this in a completely different way. We're [. . .] pissed off, right? They're in our airspace, our airspace, and we control our air, right? Think of that concept. Maybe it's the opposite—maybe we're in their airspace, right, and they're concerned because the air was their territory, or the deep sea was their territory and now we've penetrated it in the 20th century for the first time."

But the most important reason to compare UAP and shamanic experiences is the oddly specific ways they overlap:

illness-related callings, intimate interactions in liminal spaces with trickster beings who are both terrifying and seductive, encounters with anomalous spirit animals, and transformative aftermaths marked by the acquisition of occult knowledge and healing gifts.

To fully appreciate this, compare the eighteenth-century "Guests from the Sky" (in our "Sightings" section) with Chris Bledsoe's in his 2023 memoir *UFO of God*. Both carry unusual credibility. Ji Yun, a government official and leading scholar, intimately investigated his friend Tiechan's case. Bledsoe's memoir features forewords from former CIA officer Jim Semivan and Colonel John B. Alexander, plus documented visits from NASA scientists and Pentagon investigators who have personally observed aspects of his experiences.

Despite being written hundreds of years apart in different cultures, their narrative patterns line up to a surprising degree as well. During Bledsoe's Cape Fear River encounter, he and others present experienced missing time after encountering luminous orbs. Through pieced-together memories, Bledsoe later recalled meeting beings of light in a craft, including a feminine entity he calls rather archetypally "the Lady" who thereafter regularly visited him. Like Tiechan's ongoing relationship with the xian nü immortal depicted in "Guests from the Sky" within the confines of a floating orb (and like the accounts of many recent experiencers), Bledsoe's contact continues for an extended time, through both involuntary abductions and voluntary communion, during both dreams and waking states.

Both men's encounters follow intense illness. Tiechan's experience begins with a long illness and subsequent hunting retreat in the Xian mountains as he seeks to restore his health. Bledsoe, a former successful contractor, had his encounter after an unenviable trifecta of severe Crohn's disease, a near-death experience from mis-prescribed medication, and financial devastation. In a *Coast to Coast* interview, he recalls: "I was at the bottom of my barrel [. . .] crying out to God: help me, what do I do, how do I feed my kids?"

These dire straits are relevant because shamanic callings frequently begin with what religious historian Mircea Eliade calls "shamanic illness"—an intense crisis, severe illness, or bout of madness experienced as a kind of personal death. Suffering, in other words, is the admission price we pay to enter the theater of the gods. This is because it triggers altered states of consciousness, thus fulfilling the same psychological function as more intentional practices. As the Sufi poet Rumi puts it, "The wound is the place where the Light enters you."

When the mind is cracked open, shamanic encounters with spirit guides can begin. Eliade outlines what follows: "The content of these first ecstatic experiences [. . .] almost always includes [. . .] ascent to the sky and dialogue with the gods or spirits, [or] descent to the underworld and conversations with spirits and souls of dead shamans." Newly initiated shamans, in other words, can physically or spiritually travel to domains beyond ordinary perception because they can now see the exit ramp. And perhaps, in becoming aware of these places, their inhabitants become aware of them as well.

Tiechan's ascent (referred to as "soul flight" in shamanism) unfolds exactly this way. The rotating orbs, which he perceives even with closed eyes (suggesting consciousness alteration rather than just mere visual phenomena), open to reveal female beings. They levitate him upward to a strange chamber.

Bledsoe's soul flight too includes being taken aboard a craft. Like Tiechan, he meets a female entity who is overwhelmingly powerful and beautiful. Most remarkably, the descriptions of the orbs they both encounter are strongly reminiscent of not just each other but other modern accounts. In the Wudang Mountains in China, for example, orbs are frequently witnessed that move with purpose and intelligence. These are identified as immortals or "ling" (cultivated spirits) and are said to also become visible during advanced stages of meditation and qigong practice. Similarly, in the Australian outback, we have orbs such as the Min Min lights which some Australian aboriginals interpret as ancestral spirits. Bledsoe's "angelic energy beings" (he is convinced this is what they are) fit comfortably in such a spiritual taxonomy. According to him, during their long acquaintance, he has seen them morph from glowing spheres in which faces can sometimes be seen to 125-foot winged entities to aircraft-like forms.

The transformative aftermath of such meetings reveals the deepest parallel between UAP encounters and shamanic experience: their spiritual nature. The FREE study, which analyzed responses from over 4000 UAP contactees across 100+ countries, recorded increased spiritual awareness, heightened ecological concerns, and healing abilities—traditional shamanic outcomes. In *The Omega Project*, Kenneth Ring, professor emeritus of psychology at the University of Connecticut, found similar shifts among abductees: reduced materialism, environmental consciousness, psychic sensitivity, and a deeper spiritual orientation.

Bledsoe's transformation follows this positive pattern too, showing heightened spiritual abilities and a teacher's dedication to sharing his experiences. Tiechan's case, however, is trickier, despite his pre-existing engagement with the occult. He undergoes a dramatic shamanic-like change, yet it is far from positive. In fact, it proves deadly. But the two accounts don't actually diverge here. Negative transformation is transformation nevertheless, and negative outcomes are well documented across shamanic literature, just as negative near-death experiences occur.

In fact, shamanic traditions recognize and warn against "soul loss"—where portions of the self become disconnected or damaged during spiritual journeying if proper techniques aren't followed or undertaken with the proper "heart," leading to psychological fragmentation, psychosis, coma, and death.

Tiechan's destructive transformation may then be read as stemming from his wrong motivation—the egoistic pursuit of immortality through occult dabbling rather than spiritual service. His death represents what shamanic traditions call the dangers of unprepared contact with otherworldly forces and mirrors warnings frequently given to other spiritual explorers: whether psychonauts, Ouija dabblers, or artists tempted to stare too deeply into Nietzsche's void.

Therefore, ultimately both accounts follow the shamanic template: crisis-altered consciousness, otherworldly contact, and profound transformation. This reveals the utility of looking at UAP experiences through a shamanic framework. That said, the shared characteristics overviewed here barely scratch the surface. The two categories of experiences also share themes of dismemberment (and surgical variations of the idea of being taken apart and put back together); erotic encounters, spirit wives and children, implantation of foreign objects, and most unsettling of all—the recognition that we occupy a middle rung in the great chain of being, as far beneath certain non-human intelligences as insects are beneath us. As the African shaman Malidoma Patrice Somé counsels, "[W]e are often watched from a close distance by beings we ourselves cannot see, and [. . .] when we do see these otherworldly beings, it is only after they have given us permission to see further [. . .]"

18. SYMBOLIC THOUGHT, METAPHYSICAL QR CODES, AND UFOS

Reading UAPs as symbolic phenomena has become increasingly common in UAP studies, from Jung's view of them as "psychoid" events (phenomena that exist simultaneously in both psychic and physical reality) to Diana Walsh Pasulka's observation in *American Cosmic* that UFOs function as hierophanies, manifestations of the sacred in the modern world that invite both interpretation and participation.

Therefore, understanding how symbols and symbolic thought work is essential for UAP research. Besides, we are deeply symbolic creatures, from our mohawks and mullets to our butterfly tattoos, pride flags, and MAGA hats. Even our scientific language is packed with metaphors. This is seen when physicists discuss gravity in terms of "attraction" and talk about "the pull of heavenly bodies" as if the universe were both a little bit lonely and a little bit horny.

Such symbols are more than simple linguistic ornaments. Through them, the imaginative, the psychological, and the physiological entangle in fascinating ways. Red doesn't just "mean" excitement or danger, for example. It sparks actual neurological arousal in the brain, making us more alert. That's why a red light glowing in darkness feels charged with energy, why a red dress turns heads, while blue light calms the mind and slows the heart.

Research on ritualistic masks reveals even more intriguing effects. Psychologists like Hang Sun and anthropologists like Michael Winkelman have shown that donning archetypal masks—such as the ritualistic jaguar faces in Amazonian shamanism—helps trigger altered states of consciousness. Wearers report becoming the animal, spirit, or character the mask represents and speak of the mask "wearing them" rather than the reverse. This casts symbols as active technologies of consciousness, a fact well known to artists and shamans as well as proponents of "dress for success."

Conceptual Metaphors

Magic too lies in how profoundly conceptual metaphors organize experience beneath conscious awareness. As linguists George Lakoff and Mark Johnson have shown, when we talk about "being at a crossroads" in relationships, "going our separate ways," or "hitting a dead end," we're mapping love onto journeys without realizing it. In arguments, we "attack weak points," "get shot down," and have claims declared "indefensible"—treating ideas like warfare. Alternatively, we might frame our interaction with knowledge as food: consuming "raw facts," chewing on "half-baked ideas," and rejecting "warmed-over theories."

Recent research by cognitive psychologists Thibodeau and Boroditsky demonstrates how even framing crime as a "beast" versus a "disease" dramatically shifts public policy preferences toward punishment versus rehabilitation. Essentially, our underlying metaphors act as stealth programming, unconscious frameworks that shape how we treat others and what aspects of ourselves we cultivate. They determine how we practice religion or medicine, conduct business, parent, how we love, and relate to the environment. We don't just interpret symbols. We live them.

Metaphysical QR Codes

Ancient thinkers laid the groundwork for exploring this. They recognized that, just as we can see only 0.0035% of the electromagnetic spectrum, our everyday perception takes in only a fraction of reality. Symbolic perception was their technology for accessing the rest. As a result, they treated symbols as metaphysical QR codes, patterns that, when properly scanned by consciousness, unlocked access to hidden dimensions of meaning and being.

This is implied in the very etymology of the word "symbol." Historian Peter Struck points out that the Greek word "symbolon" originally denoted one half of an object split between parties in an agreement, later reassembled to verify the deal. The word also described passwords or tokens allowing entry into secret places. Symbols reunited what had been separated, functioned as passwords into hidden realms, and required consciousness and intention to work.

All these implications are at play in Plato's famous Theory of Forms. It presents this world as imperfect shadows cast by a higher, more perfect order of reality. For Plato, this deep reality is ordinarily hidden, like code running software or pixels composing an image. But through proper intellectual training, we can glimpse this deeper generative realm. In his model too, a beautiful object doesn't just represent Beauty. It echoes, manifests, and participates in the Form of Beauty. This somewhat elusive idea can be easily understood if one thinks of a Platonic form as an underlying energetic pattern or frequency one can come into resonance with. As Nikola Tesla famously advocated, if you want to find the secrets of the universe, think in terms of energy, frequency, and vibration.

While this multidimensional view of reality might seem like one of the many odd convictions haunting the drafty castle walls of history, such thinking continues to inform our brightest minds. Mathematical physicist Roger Penrose, awarded the 2020 Nobel Prize in Physics for his work on black holes, openly describes himself as a modern Platonist. In *The Road to Reality*, he argues that mathematical forms and truths exist in a real, non-physical dimension our minds can access and that we discover, rather than invent, mathematical truths. And Carl Jung, rather than seeing ideas as self-generated, views them instead as something like animals in a forest or people in a room, encountered when we connect to the vast field of consciousness underlying material reality. Such moments of contact led Jung to realize, as he reflects in his memoir *Memories, Dreams, and Reflections*: "that there is something in me which can say things that I do not know and do not intend." Contemporary reports of "downloading" experiences or information during UAP encounters extend this idea.

Correspondence

Approaching the world symbolically enables us to perceive how everything reflects everything else. The ancient Hindu-Buddhist metaphor of Indra's net captures such interconnection perfectly: an infinite web stretching across all of space, with a brilliant, perfectly reflective jewel at every intersection. Each jewel reflects all the others in the net, so that peering into any single jewel reveals not only every other jewel but their reflections in one another, creating infinite depth and connection.

The entire universe appears complete within each point—every individual event contains and communicates the whole; the emotional reflects the physical; the human the plant; the earthly the cosmic; and the world we encounter reflects our mind.

The Swiss mystic Swedenborg, who inspired Romantics from Blake to Emerson, developed a similar understanding of cosmic correspondence. Swedenborg taught that everything in the natural world corresponds to something in the spiritual world, with material objects functioning as concretized metaphors and nexus points where divine energies might "inflow" and become visible. Light is both a physical phenomenon and correspondence for wisdom; warmth is both heat and love.

Such resonance-based thinking appears throughout Asian thought, from Traditional Chinese Medicine to I Ching divination and Lu Ji's *The Art of Writing* (c. 289 CE). Ralph Waldo Emerson, inspired by both Western and Eastern traditions, distilled the correspondence view in his essay "Nature": "Every natural fact is a symbol of some spiritual fact." Thus, the sunrise embodies renewal and awakening awareness, not just the beginning of another day. Ocean waves reveal the rhythmic breathing of a larger consciousness and our connection to this underlying transcendental unity, not merely the movement of water. Imagination itself becomes what Emerson called "a very high sort of seeing."

And what one sees is that the universe works like a beautifully written book and that the creation of literature is in fact metaphysical training, a way to sharpen our spiritual awareness at the same time it is also a fractal reflection of a vaster cosmic process.

The drama theorist Bert States once asked: Why don't we interpret everyday life like we interpret the events of dreams? For Swedenborg and Emerson, you would.

Manifestation

Symbolic thought gets stranger still. Many of us act as if symbols don't just enable perception of reality's subtle dimensions but actively connect us to, resonate with, and draw down energy from more energetic realms, whether these are conceived as inner, higher, or simply multidimensional.

This talismanic conviction leads us to cite holy verses for protection, wear crosses or mala beads, take communion, visualize outcomes, or—if you live in Pennsylvania like us—mount "barn stars" on our houses to summon luck and repel evil.

The Chinese Taoist Fu tradition is another great example of such a practice. Fu talismans consist of complex characters or sacred symbols usually written on yellow paper. They are designed to channel and also shape qi (the universal life force from which all existence manifests). But they don't work automatically. One's intention and altered state of consciousness—via meditative brush strokes, ritual chants, and stirred-up emotions—are crucial to tapping into the underlying energy field and transforming such characters into batteries of spiritual power and containers of spirit intention (*shenyi*, 神意). Thus, the Fu talismans are largely focusing instruments. Taoist practice also emphasizes that symbols used repeatedly build up power over time, like a battery being charged, making them easier to use.

Contemporary Western comic artists attest to similar manifestation principles playing out in their work. Jeffrey Kripal explores this in *Mutants, Mystics, and Superheroes*, documenting how comic creators repeatedly experience synchronicities between their graphic art and reality.

In 1970s Los Angeles, for example, Doug Moench was writing a scene for a *Planet of the Apes* comic about a black-hooded gorilla named Brutus invading the human hero's home, grabbing the man's mate by the neck, and holding a gun to her head. Just as Moench finished this scene, his wife called to him from across the house. He walked toward her from their living room only to encounter a man in a black hood with one arm around his wife's neck and the other holding a gun to her head.

"It was exactly what I had written," Moench told Kripal. "It was so immediate in relation to the writing and such an exact duplicate of what I had written that it became an instant altered state. The air in the room congealed, became almost like fog, and yet, paradoxically, I could see with greater clarity."

In an interview with *SuicideGirls*, comic book writer Grant Morrison describes similar "hypersigil" manifestations when writing *The Invisibles*. "I got so enmeshed [. . .] that I was producing holographic voodoo effects and found that I could make stuff happen just by writing about it," Morrison recalls. When he wrote the character King Mob's face eaten away by bacteria, Morrison's own face became infected. And when Morrison wrote about a character dying, Morrison nearly died of blood poisoning in the hospital, deciding then to write his character out of trouble, using the image-text to heal himself.

Morrison also adopted a daily practice of making sigils, writing down what he wanted to manifest, then crossing out duplicate letters and making the text gradually more abstract until he had a sufficiently occult-looking symbol that he could charge and visualize when in the appropriate state of consciousness.

Key here is creating the sigil while in a state of "magical consciousness," a meditative state similar to that in which Fu talismans are made and that Zen koans are meant to trigger.

Morrison writes in his essay "Pop Magick": "Magical consciousness is a particular way of seeing and interacting with the real world. I experience it as what I can only describe as a 'head-click,' a feeling of absolute certainty accompanying a perceptual shift which gives real world transactions the numinous, uncanny feeling of dreams."

Morrison describes this as a heightened state similar to "some drug trips" where "many apparently precognitive and telepathic latencies become more active." He concludes that "this is the state in which tea leaves are read, curses are cast, goals are scored, poems are written."

Such "reflective" synchronicities aren't confined to comic creators. We routinely hear similar accounts in connection with pure-text fiction from fellow writers. Even arch-skeptic Mark Twain provided several examples in his 1891 essay "Mental Telegraphy." In one case, Twain conceived an idea for a book about Nevada silver mines and wrote a detailed letter to William H. Wright proposing the project. He never sent the letter. But seven days later, he received a letter from Wright dated the same day Twain had written his, proposing the exact same book with identical structure and sequence.

Twain experienced so many "letter crossings" in fact that he developed a "superstition," essentially a manifestation practice. "When I get tired of waiting upon a man whom I very much wish to hear from, I sit down and compel him to write... I [next] write him, and then tear my letter up, satisfied that my act has forced him to write me at that same moment." Twain was particularly fascinated by whether we can actively trigger correspondences rather than merely observing them, demonstrating how the lines between precognition and manifestation can blur. This is seen as well in cultural artifacts from the infamous precognitive episodes of *The Simpsons* to Ryo Tatasuki's manga *The Future I Saw*.

UAPs and Symbols

Everything discussed here, from the neurological effects of

color to comic book manifestations, points to how consciousness, meaning, and matter interpenetrate in ways more significant than ordinarily recognized. This interplay has increasingly come to occupy center stage in UAP studies.

For some, this means regarding UAPs as both physical facts and living symbols of deeper transcendental truths. For others, it means investigating how UAP appearances are events literally and mysteriously shaped by an individual's psyche, or how they constitute evidence that we exist in a simulation through which UAPs can phase between energetic and material forms, like divers putting on suits.

Some of the most interesting speculations use the lens of contemporary technologies. For example, former Pentagon AATIP director Luis Elizondo and Jesuit lawyer Daniel Sheehan have documented recovered UAP materials bearing "hieroglyphic-like symbols," something seen on other UAPs, such as the 1965 Kecksberg, PA UAP. This has led to theories that these symbols might act as sigil-circuits, designed to hold energy and interface with or alter consciousness.

Variations of holographic theory have become popular as well. Both Apollo 14 astronaut Edgar Mitchell's quantum hologram theory and Michael Talbot's holographic universe theory take this approach, as does the CIA report on its Gateway process experiment. This report conceives of reality as a "universal hologram" composed of interacting energy fields, which in turn are part of a limitless, undifferentiated field underlying all existence, referred to as "the Absolute"—the Tao-like mother of all things. According to this model, what we experience as physical reality is actually our body-and-culture inflected consciousness decoding holographic information from a deeper, unified field of Matrix-like energy, much like a computer reading data and projecting it as a desktop interface we can navigate. UAPs are therefore phenomena arising from the intersection of human awareness with other intelligences operating within the holographic matrix, intelligences that might never have had a physical form or that shed it long ago. Encountering them might involve shifting our awareness from ordinary reality to the holographic substrate beneath.

Regardless of one's favored speculation, it's clear that ancient symbolic traditions are important areas for exploration in UAP research and post-disclosure humanities. Whether or not one thinks of UAPs as "real" phenomena or simply as fascinating examples of living folklore, they offer an opportunity to think about the many ways we deeply engage with reality through symbols as human beings.

19. MULTI-STORIED HOUSES: MYTHOLOGICAL ENGINEERING AND UAPS

Stories haunt our worlds, I tell my writing and literature students.*

First date? You swap narratives to get to know each other—five or six defining tales that map your reality and your "you." Job interview questions extract stories. *In a news story about your life, what would the headline be? What would the person who likes you least in the world say about you? What is the biggest risk you've taken?*

Court proceedings and recent exes weaponize stories. Companies tell them on the back of their packaging. Legacy media and historians war over which stories are true. Overwhelmed by competing narratives, you go to a therapist who gives you another story in the form of a diagnosis and some useful tactics for "reframing."

These stories ripple with power. Research confirms that even fictional stories literally rewire neural architecture. In a landmark 2004 study, Dr. Joanne Cantor asked 530 undergraduates to write about frightening media experiences. Overwhelmingly,

---

* John Yu Branscum speaks for the duration of this note.

they chose childhood horror films over news coverage of real-world catastrophes such as 9/11. Movies like *Poltergeist* and *Jaws* had fundamentally altered their psychological landscape, leaving them unable to sleep alone and afraid to swim in open water for years.

During the COVID-19 pandemic, Dr. Coltan Scrivner discovered that such fictional simulation pays dividends when it comes to real-world horrors. Horror fans showed significantly greater psychological resilience than non-fans, having unconsciously practiced emotional responses to threat scenarios through fiction (dream researchers point out that such rehearsal is also a primary function of dreams).

Even brief narrative labels can trigger lasting behavioral changes. Stanford psychologist Dr. Carol Dweck's research showed that students labeled "smart" (a fixed mindset narrative) versus those told their "effort was impressive" (a growth mindset narrative) behave dramatically differently when facing challenges. Students labeled "smart" avoid difficult tasks to preserve their identity as intelligent, while students praised for effort show greater persistence and better performance on subsequent tasks.

And then there's the ever-mysterious placebo effect. The placebo effect demonstrates narrative's power in more physiological terms. Harvard Medical School's Ted Kaptchuk showed in multiple studies that simply believing in a treatment—whether it's a pill, a ritual, or a healing story—triggers the brain to release its own pharmacy of endorphins and dopamine, easing pain and improving symptoms in conditions ranging from depression to asthma.

A 2022 *Psychology Today* article overviews research on even more striking cases. Orthopedic surgeon Bruce Moseley found that fake knee surgeries worked as well as real ones in his osteoarthritis cases, Christina Draganich and Kristi Erdal discovered that thinking you slept better improves cognitive test performance, and Liron Rozenkrantz demonstrated that sniffing what patients thought was a "creativity-enhancing scent" boosted creative performance.

Stories are strange, powerful technology—consciousness-altering, brain-rewiring simulation machines. However, we've lived with them so long we've forgotten how bizarre they are.

Take reading a short story. Symbols on pulped tree hypnotize you, then teleport you out of your present reality into an alternate universe wearing someone else's skin. There, you cry real tears, laugh real laughs, and feel the whole spectrum of human emotion that you would in your "everyday" world, often more intensely. A *Matrix*-like experience without the need for advanced technology.

While I couldn't have articulated such things as a child, I was nevertheless fascinated by stories. Children, of course, are mad for them. Not just written or filmed but as filtered through play, costumes, art, or experimenting with personas and names. And just like the adults they become, they relish the power rush that comes from manipulating others' realities through narrative and practical jokes. But my fascination ran deeper.

My mom belonged to an apocalypse-minded church that published *The Plain Truth*, a monthly magazine that decoded contemporary events' secret meanings and included, as a special kicker, ongoing predictions about the world's end date. We inhabited a church-storied world, a quite anxious one at that and distinctly different from that of my classmates. We had our own holy days, language, history, you name it. No wonder we were always told: "Be in the world, but not of it."

This experience brought me to think about how just claiming that a famous historical person lived in a house could persuade you to pay an entry fee to see the inside or transformed how a space felt. How nasty rumors changed your impression of someone, and how, even if the rumor was later proven false, a story trace remained so that seeing them the same as before became impossible.

Awe at story's power led me not just to write poems but to try my hand at real-world storying. One summer in our Section 8 apartment in Shively, KY, I went to Caufield's costume store and bought the necessary ingredients to make myself a convincing werewolf: liquid latex, costume hair, facial prosthetics. Then nightly raids through the apartment complex began. Within weeks, my goal was achieved, at least temporarily. I had created my own urban legend. Though I wouldn't have termed it as such at the time, this was an early exercise in "mythological engineering."

The Technology of Belief

Mythological engineering is the deliberate creation or deployment of myths, stories that fundamentally structure our sense of self and reality. These stories typically center on unsettling events that strike at pre-rational parts of our psyche because that's where, as Sigmund Freud pointed out, powerful emotions like fear or love live. It doesn't matter whether such myths are true, partly true, or entirely made up—just that they are stories with this kind of power.

Mythological engineering isn't always intentional. One of the most famous historical cases (and a harbinger of today's collapse of trust in the media) is the 1938 *War of the Worlds* broadcast. On October 30, 1938, Orson Welles' radio adaptation of H.G. Wells' novel demonstrated narrative's power to create alternate perceptions of reality. Structured as breaking news bulletins depicting an alien invasion, the broadcast caused panic among some listeners who believed an actual Martian attack was underway, illustrating how media formats and narrative techniques could blur the line between fiction and reality, something that has assumed even greater relevance with the advent of AI technology.

Beyond such "accidental" cases, mythological engineering also gets deployed intentionally, increasingly so throughout the late 20th and 21st centuries. A dramatic example of this is the U.S. military's psychological warfare campaign, "Operation Wandering Soul," aka "Ghost Tape #12," deployed during the Vietnam War.

Military PsyOp specialists exploited Vietnamese beliefs about violent death creating dangerous spirits, especially when death occurred far from home without proper burial, and undertook a campaign designed to haunt the minds of Viet Cong soldiers. Military experts and South Vietnamese voice actors spent weeks layering Buddhist funeral music, eerie sounds, and distorted "dead soldier" voices to unsettle already exhausted fighters so much that they fled their uncanny posts for home.

Broadcast nightly from helicopters, planes, or jungle speakers near enemy positions, the recordings proved devastatingly effective, early proof that psychological operations could weaponize the metaphysical.

Cold War era government agencies continued exploring mythological engineering. Military technology historian Sharon Weinberger documents in *The Imagineers of War* the Defense Advanced Research Projects Agency's thirteen-year "Project AGILE," which included psychological warfare and mind control experiments. Weinberger describes a "Voice of God" weapon that projects voices with such clarity they seem to originate inside one's head, weaponizing divine voices. Jacques Vallée, among others, has made claims about proposals for advanced holographic or other visual technology to simulate the second coming of Christ over Cuba, creating religious panic among the Catholic population to facilitate a U.S. invasion.

While debate continues about whether these ideas ever went beyond the planning stage, the Vietnamese operation established precedent and a willingness to "go there." So it's not out of the realm of possibility. And this backdrop makes Ronald Reagan's 1987 United Nations quip particularly intriguing: "I occasionally think how quickly our differences worldwide would vanish if we were facing an alien threat from outside this world."

Given all this, it is no surprise that by the 2000s, UAP circles widely theorized that some UAP encounters are engineered, either as psychological experiments in social control or misdirection from secret military projects. And Dr. Steven Greer, founder of the Disclosure Project, has assembled hundreds of military and government witnesses testifying to a transnational cell manufacturing and staging UFO events for decades.

Such operations, if real, don't preclude non-human intelligences being involved in some encounters, however. Greer in fact believes both exist, as does journalist Ross Coulthart. Other mythological engineering theorists agree as well, like researcher Bill Grabowski who discusses such operations in regard to the West Virginia Mothman event. As he points out, it's possible that institutional actors exploit existing phenomena for their own purposes, so that there are multiple layers at work, with authentic strange experiences potentially being monitored, amplified, or redirected by human agencies. This in fact mirrors how major religions have historically dealt with unorthodox paranormal experiences.

Contact Arts 101

Government mythological engineering isn't the only hypothesis discussed in the context of UAPs. It's not even, to us, the most fascinating. Some theorize non-human intelligences conduct such engineering themselves. This theory finds its genesis in Jacques Vallée's brilliant mind, a name that by now is familiar to the reader.

Vallée revolutionized UAP studies in the 1960s by proposing that UAP phenomena function as sophisticated "control systems"—theater or staged management by non-human intelligences and designed to transform human consciousness through the same imagistic and narrative tools that make great art transformational.

This might sound cryptic at first. But when you think about it, it's simply an extrapolation of common life practices, not to mention topics commonly discussed in English Studies classes. How can one use sensual imagery, metaphor, defamiliarization techniques, powerful tropes, and narrative structure to cognitively shape readers, charm dates, or convince youth to die for abstractions on distant battlefields?

This theory explains encounters' frequent absurdity: entities asking nonsensical questions, performing seemingly pointless medical examinations, delivering contradictory messages, or otherwise behaving like tricksters (as discussed in Rabbit Hole 15). Such absurdity prevents easy categorization, ensuring experiences bypass rational analysis like good poems or koans, operating directly on consciousness's deeper levels.

As further evidence, Vallée observes that while strong similarities between ancient and modern UAP accounts persist, the manifestations have evolved alongside human technology and cultural expectations: from blimp-like "airships" of the 1890s to "flying saucers" of the 1950s to shape-shifting tic-tacs today. Yet they maintain consistent psychological and symbolic functions. This adaptability suggests systems designed to remain perpetually just beyond contemporary understanding, generating continuous cognitive dissonance while avoiding dismissal as impossible.

UAPs are, in effect, the metaphysical, non-human orchestrated, philosophically serious equivalent of Shakespeare in the park, updated decade by decade. To frame it this way is also to foreground an important question. When we envision non-human intelligences, why do we automatically think of them as scientists rather than artists? Why not consider that art or aesthetics might be a bigger motivation for them than science, or that it might be a more fundamental shaping mechanism for how they think?

Vallée has a comparatively positive take on this control system "art project," seeing it as potentially a consciousness-raising operation conducted by multidimensional entities working to prod our evolution beyond tribal violence and status-seeking, a kind of cosmic koan. John Keel and others, however, argue that these intelligences have no interest in our evolution or any higher purpose (any more than humans concern themselves with the religions of birds). Rather, the entities behind these story tricks are simply alien counterparts to children playing with crawdads or flies: amoral tricksters, or scientists with a bin full of white rats.

Although biased by our professional hats perhaps, we find mythological engineering among the most compelling UAP theories. We're drawn to phenomena that seem initially esoteric but reveal themselves as counterparts to everyday practices. And we like that you can approach this theory from multiple angles, ranging from deliberate campaigns by intelligence agencies to consciousness technology wielded by non-human intelligences.

As well, it invites us to think deeply about how fundamentally storytelling shapes our world. This question has only grown more urgent as we navigate an increasingly complex information landscape, one imprinted with others' narrative designs. Stories shape reality. There's no question about that. The only question is whether we'll write our own or remain bit players in someone else's script.

The Yellow Emperor visits me in my dreams.
It is there that he has passed on the secret teachings.
I have been warned not to reveal them to you.
If I did, the mountains would fade away,
The forests would dissolve.

—Shi Tao, artist and poet
(1641–1717)

READER'S GUIDE: DISCUSSION QUESTIONS

1. Most Convincing Cases

This book ranges from tenth-century Chinese "pearls" and wheel-ships to mass sightings, nuclear base incursions, and modern whistleblowers describing egg-shaped craft. Which specific cases—ancient or contemporary—do you personally find most convincing, and why? Is it the number and quality of witnesses, the presence of physical effects (burns, car shutdowns, radar tracks), the fit with patterns across cultures and centuries, or something harder to name—like how a story lodges in your psyche and refuses to leave?

2. Ontological Shock

One thing disclosure would bring (whether or not you think it is already happening) is ontological shock: a serious destabilizing of our sense of what reality is, how it works, and who we are and who others are too. Outside the topic of UFOs, this kind of shock hits us all the time—through personal experiences, things we learn, or sudden awakenings and satoris that rearrange everything at once.

What have been the biggest ontological shocks in your life so far? Cast your mind wide. Maybe your biggest shocks came from realizing something about human relationships or psychology. Maybe from suddenly understanding something about the nature of grief or love. Or maybe they concerned your sense of identity, the nature of divinity, or something else entirely.

3. Ways of Knowing

Today in the West, we often speak as if there were only one legitimate way to know something: formal scientific proof. But in practice most of us rely on all kinds of knowledge—through our senses, through tradition, wide reading, pattern recognition, lived experience, and listening to authorities we trust. Take for example the rather recent realization that dogs are capable of love—something well known before it was ever proven in a laboratory by measuring the release of oxytocin. Add to all this that scientific knowledge is only directly applicable to a small portion of our world: the kinds of phenomena whose variables can be isolated, controlled, and measured in relatively tidy settings, which leaves out a huge range of experiences. In contrast, many of the Asian traditions in this book treat inward gazing—inner experiments in meditation, journeying into one's own mind and emotions, moral and aesthetic practice, and even certain flow states—not just as self-care, but as a primary way of gaining inner knowledge about how reality works.

Looking at your own life, what different ways of knowing do you draw upon—sensory experience, scientific studies, careful observation over time, testimony from people you trust, intuition, dreams, synchronicities, spiritual experiences, self-examination and inward journeying, cultural assumptions, art, or something else? Which of these feel most trustworthy to you and which do you feel a bit uneasy about?

4. Crash-Retrieval Testimony

In the last few decades, a growing number of insiders have claimed that governments and private contractors are hiding crash-retrieval and reverse-engineering programs for non-human craft—and in some cases non-human bodies. These witnesses include intelligence officers like David Grusch, former Pentagon officials like Luis Elizondo, retired flag officers like Rear Admiral Tim Gallaudet, physicists like Hal Puthoff and Eric Davis, military pilots like David Fravor, and firsthand retrieval operatives like Jake Barber—figures with security clearances, distinguished service records, and in several cases, sworn congressional testimony. Investigative journalists like Ross Coulthart and George Knapp have spent years corroborating their accounts. Some officials and scientists reject these claims as rumor or disinformation; others call for more hearings and declassification.

When you encounter this kind of testimony—from named officials across multiple governments rather than anonymous internet posts—what counts as enough to take it seriously for you: sworn statements under penalty of perjury, multiple independent witnesses, physical samples analyzed by open labs, leaked documents, official acknowledgments, or something else? Do you currently lean toward thinking that such programs probably exist, probably do not exist, or that it is too early to tell—and what specific kinds of evidence would most likely change your mind?

5. Why Would Advanced Craft Crash?

Some people argue it's absurd to imagine craft from an advanced non-human intelligence crashing at all. They contend that any civilization capable of reaching us would never make mistakes. But this assumes total control over a complex universe is possible, and that advanced beings would never face equipment failure, environmental surprises, or actions by other parties. It also ignores how many accidents we have every year with familiar technologies—thousands of aviation incidents, industrial disasters, and even hundreds of deaths from people slipping in the shower.

If you set aside the idea of perfect, error-free intelligences and assume that crashes of anomalous craft occur, what possibilities make the most sense? Genuine accidents? Side effects of operating in a difficult environment? Conflict between different groups? Staged events meant to seed us with technology, like adults giving a child a Rubik's Cube to figure out? Something else? How does your answer change the way you interpret crash-retrieval stories?

6. Motives for Secrecy

Suppose it turned out that governments have been hiding UFO crash retrievals for decades, from Roswell and earlier cases up through nuclear-era incidents. What reasons would you find most plausible and sympathetic for such secrecy (avoiding ontological shock, preventing panic, protecting classified tech, not destabilizing religion, strategic advantage, fear of admitting loss of control, maintaining control, etc.)? Which of those motives, if any, would you personally feel at peace with, and which would feel like a betrayal?

7. Fallacies

We often, somewhat ironically, secretly define confirmation bias as "a fallacy other people make." Let's work against that.

Here are some fallacies that commonly arise whenever anyone discusses paranormal, anomalous, or spiritual experiences. How many of these have you heard before, on either side of the debate? How many have you indulged in?

a. **Ad Hominem** Shifting focus from the evidence to the person reporting it—questioning their character, credentials, or motivations rather than addressing the substance of what they're claiming. Example: "They're just publishing this book about UFOs to get attention or make money" or "That scientist only rejects UFO evidence because he's protecting his academic reputation and government funding."

b. **Straw Person Arguments** Misrepresenting a claim to make it easier to refute or exaggerating it to make it more compelling. Example: "Ghost believers think every dust particle is a spirit" or "Skeptics deny all unexplained phenomena despite the evidence."

c. **Begging the Question** Assuming the conclusion in your premise. Example: "Ghosts don't exist because supernatural things aren't real" or "This must be a genuine haunting because spirits exist."

d. **Argument from Ignorance** Assuming something is false because it hasn't been proven true, or assuming something is true because it hasn't been proven false. Example: "There's no definitive proof of ESP, so it doesn't exist" or "Scientists can't explain this light in the sky, so it must be aliens."

e. **Hasty Generalization** Drawing a sweeping conclusion from too few cases. Example: "Some ghost photos were faked, so all are fake" or "This UFO video seems genuine, so all UFO reports must be true."

f. **False Dichotomy** Framing the issue as a choice between two extremes, ignoring more nuanced possibilities. Example: "Either all reports are hoaxes or they're literal proof of the supernatural" or "Either you believe all paranormal claims or you're closed-minded to possibilities beyond materialist science."

g. **Appeal to Ridicule** Presenting an opponent's argument as absurd, ridiculous, or humorous, and therefore not worthy of serious consideration. This often shows up when people feel threatened by unfamiliar ideas or cultures. Example: Person A: "At one time in prehistory, the continents were fused together into a single supercontinent, which we call Pangaea." Person B: "Oh sure, and I bet a giant laser sliced it apart!" Or: "So what if multiple military pilots reported unusual aerial phenomena? What's next, they start claiming Elvis and Bigfoot are running a taco stand on Mars?"

h. **Appeal to Consequences** Arguing something shouldn't be believed or taken seriously because it would lead to undesirable outcomes. Example: "If people believe in the paranormal, they'll stop caring about real issues, so we shouldn't discuss it" or "If people concern themselves with worldly matters, they'll neglect the spirit and the life of the mind."

8. Asian Worldviews

Throughout this book, we explore Asian ways of thinking that see reality as relational and ever-changing: Taoist ideas of yin–yang and hua (transformation), Chinese correlative thinking and resonance (ganying), Buddhist and yogic notions of multiple realms, both/and thinking, and Shinto images of a world crowded with kami and other presences. These traditions often treat mind and matter as two faces of one process, not two separate substances. When you compare these perspectives with the worldview you grew up with, what feels familiar and what feels radically different? Do ideas like yin–yang balance, qi, relational spirits, and kami make reality feel more plausible to you, less plausible, or just strange in a useful way? Has reading these Asian accounts shifted how you imagine what UFOs/UAPs might be—or how reality itself is put together?

9. Truths Hidden in Stories

This book not only entertains the idea that we should take ancient historical records seriously—such as the Chinese accounts in "Sightings"—but also the more radical possibility that fairy tales, religious parables, legends, and myths may carry their own kinds of truth. Not just factual clues about reality, but hints about the nature of the heart, the mind, and the structure of existence itself.

Think about the stories you grew up with—folk tales, scriptures, family legends, urban myths, favorite fantasy or ghost stories. Can you name a few that have stayed with you? Now consider: what kinds of truths might be hidden in them? Are those truths metaphorical, allegorical, psychological, spiritual, or possibly even literal in ways you once dismissed? Has reading this book made any of those old stories harder to dismiss—or stranger to revisit? And do you think any of these stories might have shaped your sense of the world?

10. Layered Selves

Across Asia and the West, thinkers keep circling a similar hunch: a human being is not one solid "I," but many selves—

each one you, yet not quite you. Some exist only with certain others. Some live in different organs—a heart-self, a mind-self, a genital-self. Some appear only in certain places, like the self that emerges walking alone in the woods, synced to the rhythm of movement and nature. Some are sparked into being by a song or a scent.

Indian texts like the Upanishads, for example, speak of layered sheaths (koshas)—a physical body, a breath-energy body, a thinking-feeling mind, and a quieter, deeply peaceful layer resting near an underlying great silence (if you close your eyes and feel down into yourself, you may sense a hint of this). Buddhist and especially Tibetan teachings distinguish ordinary waking awareness from dream consciousness, deep sleep, and even subtler modes of knowing, yet insist that no single state is the one "true" self.

Elsewhere, in Chinese thought, every person has a lighter, heavenly hun soul and a heavier po or body-soul; at death the hun rises and the po dissolves back into the earth, becoming a ghostly residue of the body. Greek philosophers and storytellers add further divisions: the everyday psyche, a daimon or guiding inner spirit, and an eidolon, a ghostly image or shade. Even neuroscience finds multiplicity: when surgeons sever the connection between brain hemispheres, each half can develop its own perspective, its own story about who "I" am.

Contemporary psychology distinguishes conscious from unconscious, public from private selves, speaks of inner children and internalized mother-voices, and notices how different "you" can be in different roles and relationships. Even your dreams hint at this layering: all night long you inhabit a dream-self who loves, fears, travels, and sometimes dies, and then you wake up relieved to "come back" to your daytime life. In everyday life, you slip between selves without thinking: the body that aches and ages, the persona you present at work, the version of you that exists only with certain people, and those earlier selves who still live inside—who you were at two, at twelve, at twenty-two —each one still speaking in your head.

In how many different ways do you actually experience yourself—physically, emotionally, socially, spiritually, ecologically, online, in dreams, in memory? Which of these selves feel most real or alive to you, and which feel thinner or more artificial? Are there moments when one self seems to take over completely, or times when you sense several selves operating at once?

11. Dimensions of Existence

The proposition that there are multiple dimensions sounds a bit wild or woo at first hearing. But most traditions and sciences acknowledge multiple dimensions of existence. An intellectual history of humanity in fact reveals the perpetual discovery of new dimensions: the microscopic, the quantum, the unconscious, the macrocosmic, the underwater, the digitally delineated, the lucidly dreamed. So the real question isn't if reality is multidimensional, but which multiple dimensions each of us believes in, and which we have trouble believing in.

What "dimensions" of existence do you recognize? Try to name and number them. And how many of these dimensions of existence do you think might be inhabited in some way—and by what?

12. An Ecology of Beings

Many who take UAPs and other anomalies seriously no longer picture just one type of non-human intelligence, but a whole ecology: nuts-and-bolts extraterrestrials, time-traveling future humans, plasma- or field-based species, trickster-like ultraterrestrials, AI hive minds, nature spirits, spiritual entities, and more. Indeed, several anecdotes and people in this book lean toward a multi-layered cosmos crowded with overlapping forms of mind. Which kinds of non-human intelligences strike you as most plausible, and why? Which are hardest for you to buy into—and what tips the scales for you: scientific constraints, philosophical arguments, cultural or religious commitments, or your own boggle threshold about how strange reality is allowed to be?

13. How Malleable is Your Perception?

Many accounts in this book suggest that UAPs and non-human entities may stay hidden not only through advanced technology and the limits of our instruments, but by manipulating human perception itself—or by exploiting how our minds already filter reality.

How malleable do you think your own perception is? When have you discovered your senses or memories were wrong—optical illusions, misheard lyrics, gaslighting, déjà vu, intense dreams, social media narratives that turned out to be false?

What strategies seem most useful for resisting false beliefs, false memories, and engineered perceptions—mechanical ones (cameras, multiple witnesses, journaling) or psychological ones (critical thinking, peer review, cross-cultural comparison)? Which do you actually use? And have you ever manipulated someone else's perception—and did it work?

14. Ethics, Consent, and Power

Many of the encounters in this book, and in modern reports, sit in an unsettling space between awe and violation. Some people describe contact with non-human intelligences as healing, loving, or initiatory; others experience it as invasive, terrifying, or traumatizing, with memories of paralysis, forced procedures, or having their lives quietly monitored. These mixed reports raise uncomfortable questions about power, consent, and ethics.

When you think about human–"alien" encounters, do they feel to you more like friendship and teaching, more like experimentation and tagging (the way humans tranquilize, collar, and track animals), or something stranger that doesn't fit either model?

If you imagine that non-human intelligences really are studying us, what ethical standards—if any—do you think they should follow?

And turning the mirror around, does thinking about these encounters change how you feel about the way humans use animals or other forms of life in labs, zoos, and studies, or about our right to observe and experiment on other beings at all?

15. Sexual Encounters and Consciousness

A few sections in this book explore intimacy with non-human entities and go so far as to frame it as a kind of "interface technology" for consciousness and information exchange. If it were possible to enter into a sexual or intimate relationship with a non-human intelligence—whether extraterrestrial or multidimensional; spirit, angel, fairy, or immortal—would you be curious, horrified, tempted, or something else entirely? More personally, have you ever had an erotic experience that seemed to shift your consciousness in some way, and how does it do so?

16. Life After Disclosure

A humanities approach to people's accounts of UFO experiences treats them less as things to be proven or debunked and more as sources of meaning: stories, symbols, traumas, and spiritual experiences that reorganize how individuals think about consciousness, reality, and our place in the universe and on the food chain—no matter how factual we personally think such stories are. A post-disclosure humanities approach additionally asks how culture, beliefs, and identity are transformed when "we are not alone" becomes a basic social fact.

Piggybacking off Ted Peters' 2011 ETI Religious Crisis Survey—which asked over 1,300 religious and non-religious respondents how confirmation of extraterrestrial intelligence would affect their beliefs—how do you think the following would change? (Choose two or three.)

a) How we understand ourselves and our place in the cosmos b) Religious beliefs and practices c) How we treat other humans, animals, and the environment d) Trust in government, media, and institutions e) How we understand perception and consciousness f) How we read history g) Any other area you think would be most transformed

17. Aliens in Popular Culture

Keeping in mind both the ancient and modern UAP-related lore and accounts in these pages, which movies, TV series, games, or works of literature do you think come closest to "getting aliens right"—and what, exactly, do they get right? Is it their behavior, their motives, their effect on human consciousness and society, the weirdness of the encounters themselves, or something else? And which popular depictions do you think get it most wrong—and what do they miss?

AFTERWORD

Stars That Pause is the third book in our exploration of Asian records of the strange, a journey that began with *The Shadow Book of Ji Yun*, a project undertaken out of our love for and delight in such material. In that book, we wanted to lay bare the roots of contemporary speculative fiction—from K-dramas to anime. In this present volume, we likewise approach UAPs not as divorced from other human concerns, but as deeply interwoven with them. This reflects an Asian worldview that sees all aspects of existence as interconnected, each reflecting the others, so that even readers uninterested in UFOs might find something in these pages to spark their curiosity beyond the specific topic.

This book is also a thought experiment, inspired by NASA-funded Princeton studies asking theologians across religions to imagine how their theologies would look after disclosure. In a similar vein, as we wrote, we continually asked ourselves: What would the humanities look like if the universe turns out stranger than we thought? How might our field's core concerns —language, meaning-making, storytelling, inhabiting the world

—engage with phenomena that fundamentally unsettle our deepest convictions about humanity's place in the cosmos? How do we discuss such phenomena? What else must we discuss alongside them? How do they connect to human history, psychology, and even the nature of physical intimacy? These questions guided us as much as our sustained dive into Asian UFO encounters.

Stars That Pause, then, is the first volume of our small contribution to the trailblazing work begun by so many others in UAP studies, and we eagerly look forward to future works that will follow: country-specific studies on India or Japan, tradition-specific work exploring Tibetan Buddhism's relationship to UFOs, comparisons with global NDE studies and other anomalous phenomena.

Thank you so much for your time reading this book. We hope it sparks an idea or two for your own journey down rabbit holes.

And wormholes, too.

SELECTED BIBLIOGRAPHY

Abrahams, Brad, director. *Love and Saucers*. The Orchard, 2017.
Alexander, John B. *UFOs: Myths, Conspiracies, and Realities*. New York: Thomas Dunne Books, 2011.
"Alien Encounters: An Interview with Professor Diana Pasulka." *The Thinker's Garden*, November 25, 2023. https://thethinkersgarden.com/alien-encounters-interview-with-professor-diana-pasulka/
Andreeva, Anna. "Medieval Shinto: New Discoveries and Perspectives." Religion Compass 4, no. 11 (2010): 679–693. https://doi.org/10.1111/j.1749-8171.2010.00243.x.
Angell, Marcia. "Drug Companies & Doctors: A Story of Corruption." *The New York Review of Books*, January 15, 2009.
Anonymous. *The Classic of Mountains and Seas*. Translated by Anne Birrell. London: Penguin Books, 2000.
Austin, Coco. Interview with WRIF Radio, October 31, 2016.
Azhazha, Vladimir. Quoted in Waugh, Rob. "Forget UFOs, Alien Hunters Say We Should Be Focusing on Unidentified Submerged Objects (USOs)." *The Daily Mail*, March 16, 2024. https://www.dailymail.co.uk/sciencetech/article-13191835/Forget-UFOs-alien-hunters-say-focusing-Unidentified-Submerged-Objects-USOs.html.
"Bandarawela, 1998." *Luck.lk*, February 5, 2020. https://luck.lk/bandarawela-1998/.
Bledsoe, Chris. *UFO of GOD: The Extraordinary True Story of Chris Bledsoe*. UFO of GOD, 2023.
Blumenthal, Ralph, Helene Cooper, and Leslie Kean. "Glowing Auras and 'Black Money': The Pentagon's Mysterious U.F.O. Program." *The New York Times*, December 16, 2017. https://www.nytimes.com/2017/12/16/us/politics/pentagon-program-ufo-harry-reid.html
Berliner, Don, comp. "The Bluebook 'Unknowns.'" National Investigations Committee on Aerial Phenomena. https://www.nicap.org/bluebook/unknowns.htm.
Bi, Yuan 毕沅, et al. *Xu Zizhi Tongjian* (续资治通鉴), 1801.
Boswell, Josh. "Military Personnel Have Been Hurt after UFO Encounters, Expert Says." *Mail Online*, April 7, 2022. https://www.dailymail.co.uk/news/article-10696303/Military-officers-suffered-injuries-UFO-encounters.html
———. "Area 51 Bombshell: Whistleblower Reveals Secret Egg-Shaped Craft."

Bourke, Angela. *The Burning of Bridget Cleary*. London: Pimlico Books, 2006.

Bruner, Jerome S. *Actual Minds, Possible Worlds*. Cambridge, MA: Harvard University Press, 1987.

Budden, Albert. *Electric UFOs: Fireballs, Electromagnetics and Abnormal States*. London: Blandford, 1998.

Bullard, Thomas E. *The Myth and Mystery of UFOs*. Lawrence: University Press of Kansas, 2010.

Campany, Robert Ford. *Strange Writing: Anomaly Accounts in Early Medieval China*. Albany, SUNY Press, 1996.

———. *To Live as Long as Heaven and Earth: A Translation and Study of Ge Hong's Traditions of Divine Transcendents*. University of California Press, 2002.

Campus, Jenn. "Spring Equinox: The Magic of the Cosmic Egg." March 18, 2024. https://jenncampusauthor.com/spring-equinox-the-magic-of-the-cosmic-egg/.

Cantor, Joanne. "'I'll Never Have a Clown in My House'—Why Movie Horror Lives On." *Poetics Today* 25, no. 2 (2004): 283–304.

Carey, Thomas J, and Donald R. Schmitt. *Witness to Roswell, 75th Anniversary Edition*. Red Wheel/Weiser, 2022.

Carter, Jimmy. Interview, "UFO Sighting in Georgia." *Atlanta Constitution*, September 14, 1973.

Chalker, Bill. "Strange Evidence." *International UFO Reporter*, Spring 1999.

———. "Dr. Kary Mullis: An Interesting Aside." *UFO Experiences*, July 2006.

———. "Exploring the Shamanism-Alien Abduction Connection." *New Dawn*, 2021.

Chan, Leo Tak-Hung. *The Discourse on Foxes and Ghosts: Ji Yun and Eighteenth-Century Literati Storytelling*. Honolulu, University of Hawai'i Press, 1998.

Cheung, Han. "Taiwan in Time: UFOs over the Skies of Taiwan." *Taipei Times*, June 23, 2024, www.taipeitimes.com/News/feat/archives/2024/06/23/2003819754.

China UFO Report (中国不明飞行物报告). http://www.ufocn.org/

Choi, Charles Q. "The Surprising Origin of Alien Abduction Stories." *NBC News*, May 7, 2012.

Choi, Chungmoo. "The Role of the Female Shaman in Korean Society." In *Shamans, Housewives, and Other Restless Spirits: Women in Korean Shamanism*, 119–125. Honolulu: University of Hawaii Press, 1985.

Christopher, Paul. *Alien Intervention: The Spiritual Mission of UFOs*. Lafayette: Huntington House Publishers, 1998.

Cixi County Chronicles, Records of Anomalies (慈溪县志 纪异篇), 1899.

Clelland, Mike. *The Messengers: Owls, Synchronicity, and the UFO Abductee.* San Antonio: Anomalist Books, 2015.

"Close Encounters at Nuclear Bases." *UFOs: Investigating the Unknown.* National Geographic. January 24, 2023.

Coast to Coast AM Official. "Taken by UFO for 4 Hours – Why NASA & CIA Watch His Backyard | Chris Bledsoe FULL STORY." YouTube video, June 11, 2025. https://www.youtube.com/watch?v=BoCIpefVpjU

Collins, Francis. *The Language of God: A Scientist Presents Evidence for Belief.* New York: Free Press, 2006.

Confucius. *The Analects.* Translated by D.C. Lau. London: Penguin Classics, 1979.

Coulthart, Ross. *In Plain Sight: An Investigation into UFOs and Impossible Science.* London: HarperCollins Publishers, 2021.

Coward, Harold. "Taoism and Jung: Synchronicity and the Self." *Philosophy East and West* 46, no. 4 (1996): 477–495.

Crowley, Aleister. *De Arte Magica. Sure Fire Press,* 1988.

De Brouwer, Wilfried. "The UAP Wave over Belgium." In *UFOs: Generals, Pilots, and Government Officials Go on the Record,* edited by Leslie Kean, 23–38. New York: Crown Publishing, 2010.

"Declassified Russian Navy Records Say Underwater UFOs are Real." *Behind the Scenes 24 News,* May 21, 2015. https://behindthescenes24news.wordpress.com/2015/05/21/declassified-russian-navy-records-say-underwater-ufos-are-real/.

Dennett, Preston. *UFOs at the Drive-In: 100 True Cases of Close Encounters at Drive-In Theaters.* Blue Giant Books, 2020.

Derr, John S., and Michael A. Persinger. "Geophysical Variables and Behavior: LXXVI. Seasonal Hydrological Load and Regional Luminous Phenomena (UFO Reports) within River Systems, the Mississippi Valley Test." Perceptual and Motor Skills 77, no. 3 (1993): 1163–1170. https://doi.org/10.2466/pms.1993.77.3f.1163

Devereux, Paul. Earth Lights Revelation: UFOs and Mystery Lightform Phenomena. London: Blandford Press, 1989.

de Vrieze, Jop. "Landmark Research Integrity Survey Finds Questionable Practices Are Surprisingly Common." Science, July 7, 2021.

Dick, Philip K. *Valis.* London: Gollancz, 2001.

Dikaryov, A. D. "Unidentified Flying Objects in Ancient China." Central Intelligence Agency (FOIA Reading Room), Document Number 0005516227. January 1998.

Dolan, Richard. "Egg Shaped UAP: What You Need to Know." YouTube video, January 22, 2025. https://www.youtube.com/watch?v=tY1Rw3MGuOo.

———. *A History of USOs: Unidentified Submerged Objects: Volume 1: From the Beginning to 1969.* Richard Dolan Press, 2025.

———. "The Hidden Story of Chinese Ufology." *Richard Dolan Members,* March

27, 2025. https://richarddolanmembers.com/ufology/the-secret-story-of-chinese-ufology-article/.

Dongo, Tom. *Mysterious Sedona*. Light Technology Publishing, 2000.

DT Next. "'UFO Visits' near Key Nuclear Installations in Tamil Nadu Baffle Experts." March 25, 2024. https://www.dtnext.in/news/tamilnadu/ufo-visits-near-key-nuclear-installations-baffle-experts-776265.

Dumsday, Travis. *The Marian Apparitions at Zeitoun: An Evidential Inquiry*. St Vladimirs Seminary Press, 2022.

Dweck, Carol S. "Carol Dweck Revisits the 'Growth Mindset'." *Education Week*, September 22, 2015. https://www.edweek.org/leadership/opinion-carol-dweck-revisits-the-growth-mindset/2015/09.

Ehrenreich, Barbara. *Living with a Wild God: A Nonbeliever's Search for the Truth about Everything*. New York: Grand Central Publishing, 2020. Originally published in 2014.

Einstein, Albert. "Introduction." In *Mental Radio* by Upton Sinclair. Hampton Roads Publishing, 2001. Originally published in 1930.

Eliade, Mircea. *The Sacred and the Profane: The Nature of Religion*. New York: Harcourt, Brace and Company, 1959.

———. *Shamanism: Archaic Techniques of Ecstasy*. Translated by Willard R. Trask. Princeton: Princeton University Press, 2004.

Elizondo, Luis. "Advanced Aerospace Threat Identification Program Report." Declassified excerpts released by the Department of Defense, 2017.

———. *Imminent: Inside the Pentagon's Hunt for UFOs*. New York: William Morrow, 2024.

———. "Ex-Pentagon Official Confirms Alien Language Exists - Lue Elizondo - DEBRIEFED ep. 24." Interview by Chris Ramsay. YouTube video, January 31, 2025. https://www.youtube.com/watch?v=WGUb1JKxBDo.

Elliot, Andrew J., and Markus A. Maier. "Color Psychology: Effects of Perceiving Color on Psychological Functioning in Humans." *Annual Review of Psychology* 65 (2014): 95–120.

Emerson, Ralph Waldo. *Nature*. Boston: James Munroe and Company, 1836.

"Episode 183: Orbs w/ Chris Bledsoe Sr." *Bledsoe Said So*, January 22, 2025. YouTube video.https://www.youtube.com/watch?v=qVUt4VzKUsM.

Eshed, Haim. "Former Israeli Space Security Chief Says Aliens Exist, Humanity Not Ready." Interview by Yedioth Ahronoth. Quoted in *The Jerusalem Post*, December 10, 2020.

Fang, Xuanling 房玄齡 et al., comp. *Book of Jin, Chronicle of Emperor Min* (晋书 愍帝纪), 648. Reprint, Beijing: Zhonghua shuju, 1974.

Faretra, Joe. "'Clearest Footage Ever Seen' of Egg-Shaped UFO as Whistleblower Says 'We're Not Alone.'" *Daily Star*, January 20, 2025. https://www.dailystar.co.uk/news/weird-news/clearest-footage-ever-seen-egg-34516063.

Feinberg, Carey. "The Placebo Phenomenon." *Harvard Magazine*, January–February 2013.

Fernandes, Joaquim, and Fina D'Armada. *Heavenly Lights: The Apparitions of Fatima and the UFO Phenomenon*. EcceNova, 2005.

France. COMETA Report: "UFOs and Defense: What Should We Prepare For?" Paris: Institut des Hautes Études de Défense Nationale, 1999.

Fravor, David. Interview by Bill Whitaker. "Navy Pilots Describe Encounters with UFOs." *60 Minutes*. CBS, May 16, 2021.

Freeman, David. "New Whistleblower Exposes Secret UFO Retrieval Programme on NewsNation." *Above the Norm News*, January 19, 2025.

Fridman, Lex. "Garry Nolan: UFOs and Aliens." YouTube video, February 6, 2022. https://www.youtube.com/watch?v=uTCc2-1tbBQ.

Frost, Natasha. "When Dozens of Korean War GIs Claimed a UFO Made Them Sick." *History*, September 13, 2018. https://www.history.com/news/korean-war-us-army-ufo-attack-illness.

Gallaudet, Tim. "Beneath the Surface: We May Learn More about UAP by Looking in the Ocean." *The White Papers of the Sol Foundation* 1, no. 1 (2024): 1–29.

Ge, Hong 葛洪. *Baopuzi* (The Master Who Embraces Simplicity). 4th century CE. Translated by James R. Ware. *Alchemy, Medicine, and Religion in the China of A.D. 320: The Nei Pien of Ko Hung*. Cambridge, MA: MIT Press, 1966.

———. *Baopuzi* (抱朴子). Collated and annotated by Wang Ming 王明. Beijing: Zhonghua shuju, 1985.

———. *Shenxian zhuan* (神仙传). Punctuated by Hu Shouwei 胡守为. Beijing: Zhonghua shuju, 2010.

Gillette, Joe. "No Enemy Contact, but Alien Contact…" The Text Message (blog). *US National Archives*, June 6, 2011. https://text-message.blogs.archives.gov/2011/06/06/no-enemy-contact-but-alien-contact/.

Glawson, Michael. "It's Time to Rethink Some Common Assumptions About UFOs." *Debrief*, May 17, 2023. https://thedebrief.org/its-time-to-rethink-some-common-assumptions-about-ufos/

Gopalakrishna, Gowri, Lex M. Bouter, Joeri K. Tijdink, et al. "Prevalence of Questionable Research Practices, Research Misconduct and Their Associated Factors Among Academic Researchers in The Netherlands." *PLOS ONE* 17, no. 2 (2022): e0263023. https://doi.org/10.1371/journal.pone.0263023.

Grabowski, Bill, interview by George Knapp. "Anomalous Activities / Secret History." *Coast to Coast AM*, May 24, 2015. https://www.coasttocoastam.com/show/2015-05-24-show/.

Green, Christopher C. "Clinical Medical Acute & Subacute Field Effects on Human Dermal & Neurological Tissues." Defense Intelligence Agency, Advanced Aerospace Weapon System Applications Program, March 2010.

Greenhill, Richard. "These People See Colors and Taste Flavors When They Orgasm." *Vice*, September 18, 2018.

Greer, Steven M., presenter. *Unacknowledged*. Directed by Michael Mazzola. The Orchard, 2017.

———. *Contact: Countdown to Transformation*. Crozet, VA: The Crossing Point, 2009.

Halt, Charles I. *The Halt Perspective*. London: Haunted Skies Publishing, 2016.

Hastings, Robert L. *UFOs and Nukes: Extraordinary Encounters at Nuclear Weapons Sites*. AuthorHouse, 2008.

Haut, Walter G. "Affidavit of Walter Haut." May 14, 1993.

———. "Sealed Affidavit of Walter G. Haut." 2002.

Haynes, Renée. "The Boggle Threshold." *Encounter*, August 1980. https://www.unz.com/print/Encounter-1980aug-00092.

Hayssen, Gail. *Living with the Sky Spirits: Spirit-Called Shamans Among the Buryat-Mongols*. San Francisco: Bluebird Publications, 2018.

Hastings, Robert. *UFOs and Nukes: Extraordinary Encounters at Nuclear Weapons Sites*. Seattle: CreateSpace, 2017.

Hellyer, Paul. "UFOs Are as Real as the Airplanes Flying Overhead." Speech at the University of Toronto, September 25, 2005.

Henderson, John B. *The Development and Decline of Chinese Cosmology*. New York: Columbia University Press, 1984.

Hernandez, Rey. *Beyond UFOs: The Science of Consciousness and Contact with Non-Human Intelligence*. Free Foundation, 2018.

———. *A Greater Reality: The New Paradigm of Nonlocal Consciousness, the Paranormal & the Contact Modalities*. Consciousness and Contact Research Institute, 2022

"'High strangeness': Brandon Fugal and Dr Travis Taylor Discuss Skinwalker Ranch." *Sky HISTORY TV Channel*. https://www.history.co.uk/shows/curse-of-skinwalker-ranch/brandon-fugal-and-dr-travis-taylor-curse-of-skinwalker-ranch-interview

Hindu Mythology. "The Cosmic Egg: Hiranyagarbha in Hindu Creation Myths." October 21, 2024. https://hindu.mythologyworldwide.com/the-cosmic-egg-hiranyagarbha-in-hindu-creation-myths/.

Hoffman, Donald D., Manish Singh, and Chetan Prakash. "The Interface Theory of Perception." *Psychonomic Bulletin & Review* 22, no. 6 (2015): 1480–1506. https://doi.org/10.3758/s13423-015-0890-8.

Ho, Hsien-jung 何顯榮. *An Investigation of Global UFO Sightings* (UFO目擊大追蹤). Taiwan UFO Society, 2003.

Hong, Mai 洪迈. *Yijian Zhi* (夷坚志), c. 1198. Punctuated by He Zhuo 何卓. Reprint, Beijing: Zhonghua shuju, 1981.

Horowitz, Mitch. *One Simple Idea: How Positive Thinking Reshaped Modern Life*. New York: Crown, 2014.

Horton, Richard. "Offline: What Is Medicine's 5 Sigma?" *The Lancet* 385, no. 9976 (April 11, 2015): 1380.

Huertas, Oscar Santa María. "UFO Dogfight Over Peru." In *UFOs: Generals, Pilots, and Government Officials Go on the Record*, edited by Leslie Kean, 39–49. New York: Crown Publishing, 2010.

Hunter, Jack. *Engaging the Anomalous: Collected Essays on Anthropology, the Paranormal, Mediumship and Extraordinary Experience*. London: August Night Press, 2018.

Huntington, Rania. *Alien Kind: Foxes and Late Imperial Chinese Narrative*. Cambridge, Harvard University Press, 2003.

Imbrogno, Philip J., and J. Allen Hynek. *Night Siege: The Hudson Valley UFO Sightings*. New York: Ballantine Books, 1987.

Inoue, Nobutaka, general editor. Contemporary Papers on Japanese Religion 4. Translated by Norman Havens. Tokyo: Institute for Japanese Culture and Classics, Kokugakuin University, 1998.

International Chinese UFO Association. "Advance Together, Overcome Difficulties, Head for Glory: Twenty Years of the International Chinese UFO Association." April 23, 2019. http://www.360doc.com/content/23/0411/17/56044943_1076064858.shtml

"Investigation of Unsolved UFO Cases in China: Close Encounters of the Third Kind (中国UFO悬案调查：第三类接触)," *Sina Tech*, January 23, 2006. http://tech.sina.com.cn/d/2006-01-23/2202827621.shtml.

Ioannidis, John P. A. "Why Most Published Research Findings Are False." *PLOS Medicine* 2, no. 8 (August 30, 2005): e124.

Ishiba, Shigeru. "Statement on Japan's Policy Toward Unidentified Flying Objects." Press Conference, Ministry of Defense, Tokyo, December 18, 2007.

Ito, J. (1998–1999). *Uzumaki*. Shogakukan.

"'It's trying to wake us up:' Hope Mills man featured in TV show about UFOs." *The Fayetteville Observer*, November 8, 2023.

"Japanese Minister O.K.'s Fighting Godzilla." *The New York Times*, December 21, 2007.

Jarrett, Christian. "What Is Sex Like for Someone with Synesthesia?" *Smithsonian Magazine*, October 29, 2013.

Jiang, Huangrong 江晃榮. *UFO: The Warning of Flying Saucers and the Riddle of Aliens (飛碟的警告與外星人的謎團)*. Taipei: Yuhu Wenhua Chubanshe, 1995.

Jiaxing Prefecture Chronicles (嘉兴府志), 1721.

Ji, Yun. *The Shadow Book of Ji Yun: The Chinese Classic of Weird True Tales, Horror Stories, and Occult Knowledge*. Translated by Yi Izzy Yu and John Yu Branscum. Empress Wu Books, 2021.

Jung, Carl G. "Foreword to the 'I Ching'" [1949]. In *Psychology and the East*, Collected Works of C.G. Jung, Vol. 11, edited by Herbert Read, Michael Fordham, and Gerhard Adler, translated by R.F.C. Hull, 589–608. Princeton: Princeton University Press, 1958.

———. *Archetypes and the Collective Unconscious*. Collected Works of C.G. Jung, Vol. 9, Part 1. Translated by R.F.C. Hull. Princeton: Princeton University Press, 1959.

———. *Flying Saucers: A Modern Myth of Things Seen in the Skies*. Translated by R.F.C. Hull. London: Routledge & Kegan Paul, 1959.

———. *Memories, Dreams, Reflections*. Translated by Richard and Clara Winston. New York: Vintage Books, 1963.

———. *Alchemical Studies*. Collected Works of C.G. Jung, Vol. 13. Edited by Herbert Read, Michael Fordham, and Gerhard Adler. Translated by R.F.C. Hull. Princeton: Princeton University Press, 1967.

———. *Psychological Types*. Collected Works of C.G. Jung, Vol. 6. Translated by R.F.C. Hull. Princeton: Princeton University Press, 1971.

———., and Wolfgang Pauli. *The Interpretation of Nature and the Psyche*. Translated by R.F.C. Hull and Priscilla Silz. New York: Pantheon Books, 1955.

Kaku, Michio. *Physics of the Impossible: A Scientific Exploration into the World of Phasers, Force Fields, Teleportation, and Time Travel*. New York: Doubleday, 2008.

———. *Physics of the Future: How Science Will Shape Human Destiny and Our Daily Lives by the Year 2100*. New York: Doubleday, 2011.

Kastrup, Bernardo. *Meaning in Absurdity: What Bizarre Phenomena Can Tell Us about the Nature of Reality*. Winchester: Iff Books, 2012.

Kean, Leslie. *UFOs: Generals, Pilots, and Government Officials Go on the Record*. New York: Crown Publishing, 2010.

Keel, John A. *Operation Trojan Horse*. New York: G.P. Putnam's Sons, 1970.

———. *The Eighth Tower*. New York: Dutton, 1975.

———. *The Mothman Prophecies*. New York: Saturday Review Press, 1975.

Kelleher, Colm A., and George Knapp. *Hunt for the Skinwalker: Science Confronts the Unexplained at a Remote Ranch in Utah*. New York: Paraview Pocket Books, 2005.

Kelly, Ned. "This Day in History: China's Qing Dynasty UFO Incident of 1892." *That's Shanghai*, September 27, 2023.

Kendall, Laurel. "Korean Shamanism: Women's Rites and a Chinese Comparison." *Senri Ethnological Studies* 11 (1982): 69–86.

Kesha. Interview with Ryan Seacrest, September 25, 2012.

"KGB UFO Files." *ABC News Prime Time Live*. Original airdate October 6, 1994.

Kirk, Robert. *The Secret Commonwealth of Elves, Fauns, and Fairies*. 1691. New York: New York Review Books Classics, 2006.

Klaassen, Frank, and Katrina Bens. "Achieving Invisibility and Having Sex with Spirits: Six Operations from an English Magic Collection c. 1600." *Opuscula* 3, no. 1 (2013): 1–14.

Knapp, George. "Testimony Submitted to the U.S. House Oversight Committee on Unidentified Anomalous Phenomena." July 26, 2023. https://static.

foxnews.com/foxnews.com/content/uploads/2023/07/George-Knapp-Congressional-Record-Submission.pdf.

Koebler, Jason. "Found: Page 25 of the CIA's Gateway Report on Astral Projection." *VICE*, March 2021. https://www.vice.com/en/article/found-page-25-of-the-cias-gateway-report-on-astral-projection/.

Komisaruk, Barry. "This Is What Your Brain Looks Like During an Orgasm." *Vox*, April 1, 2015.

Kovalyonok, Vladimir. "UFO Sighting from Salyut 6." Quoted in Leslie Kean, *UFOs: Generals, Pilots, and Government Officials Go on the Record*. New York: Crown Publishing, 2010.

Kramer, Heinrich, and James Sprenger. *Malleus Maleficarum*. 1487. Translated by Montague Summers. Reprint, New York: Dover Publications, 1971.

Kripal, Jeffrey J. *Kali's Child: The Mystical and the Erotic in the Life and Teachings of Ramakrishna*. Chicago: University of Chicago Press, 1995.

———. *Authors of the Impossible: The Paranormal and the Sacred*. Chicago: University of Chicago Press, 2010.

———. *Mutants and Mystics: Science Fiction, Superhero Comics, and the Paranormal*. Chicago: University of Chicago Press, 2011.

———. *The Super Natural: A New Vision of the Unexplained*. Chicago: University of Chicago Press, 2016.

———. *The Secret Body: Erotic and Esoteric Currents in the History of Religions*. Chicago: University of Chicago Press, 2017.

———. *The Flip: Epiphanies of Mind and the Future of Knowledge*. New York: Penguin, 2019.

———., and Elizabeth G. Krohn. *Changed in a Flash: One Woman's Near-Death Experience and Why a Scholar Thinks It Empowers Us All*. Berkeley: North Atlantic Books, 2018.

Kuhn, Thomas S. *The Structure of Scientific Revolutions*. Chicago: University of Chicago Press, 1962.

Lachman, Gary. *Dark Star Rising: Magick and Power in the Age of Trump*. New York: TarcherPerigee, 2018.

Lakoff, George, and Mark Johnson. *Metaphors We Live By*. Chicago: University of Chicago Press, 2003.

Lee, Peter H. *Sources of Korean Tradition, Vol. 1*. Columbia University Press, 1997.

Levenda, Peter. "Engaging the Phenomenon." Podcast interview, 2023.

Levin, Michael. "Patterns are Alive, and We are Living Patterns." *Institute of Art and Ideas*. August 15, 2024. https://iai.tv/articles/patterns-are-alive-and-we-are-living-patterns-auid-2919.

Lewis-Kraus, Gideon. "How the Pentagon Started Taking U.F.O.s Seriously." *The New Yorker*, 30 April 2021. https://www.newyorker.com/magazine/2021/05/10/how-the-pentagon-started-taking-ufos-seriously.

Lin, Qingquan 林青泉. *A Summoning to the Idea of the Source of Life* (生命源头的意念

呼唤) [Eastern UFOlogy (东方飞碟学): Meditations on the Cosmos (宇宙沉思录) 4]. Shaanxi Sheying Chubanshe, 1993.

Lin, Yutang. *The Wisdom of China*. London: Michael Joseph, 1944.

Liu, Dongjun. "UFO Research Must Have Chinese Characteristics." *Scientific Chinese*, no. 10 (1999): 78.

Liu, Lucy. Interview with *Us Weekly*, September 2012.

Lomas, Tim, Brendan Case, and Michael P. Masters. "The Cryptoterrestrial Hypothesis: A Case for Scientific Openness to a Concealed Earthly Explanation for Unidentified Anomalous Phenomena." *Philosophy and Cosmology* 33 (2024): 67-122. https://doi.org/10.29202/phil-cosm/33/3.

Lu, Ji 陆机. *We Fu* (文赋, The Art of Writing). In *Wen xuan* (文选), edited by Xiao Tong 萧统, 17:727-736. Beijing: Zhonghua shuju, 1977.

Lu, Ying-chung 呂應鐘, *Five Thousand Years of UFO* (UFO五千年). Taipei: Rizhen Publishing, 1997.

———. "Seven UFO Sightings Over Taiwan During the Presidential Election Period." *Epoch Times*, July 31, 2001. https://www.epochtimes.com/b5/1/7/31/n114659.htm.

Luhrmann, T. M. "Where Reason Ends and Faith Begins." *The New York Times*, July 26, 2014. https://www.nytimes.com/2014/07/27/opinion/sunday/t-m-luhrmann-where-reason-ends-and-faith-begins.html.

Luna, Tania. "Mind Over Matter: The Power of Placebo." *Psychology Today*, January 27, 2022. https://www.psychologytoday.com/us/blog/surprise/202201/mind-over-matter-the-power-placebo.

Mack, John E. *Abduction: Human Encounters with Aliens*. New York: Scribner, 2007.

Magis Center. "A Lawyer, a Journalist, and a Scientist Detail the Miracle of the Sun." August 31, 2020. https://www.magiscenter.com/blog/a-lawyer-a-journalist-and-a-scientist-describe-the-miracle-at-fatima.

Margiotta, Lucio. "UFO Changes Shape in Salento, Italy." Video filmed January 9, 2017. Featured in *The Proof Is Out There*, Season 1, Episode 7. A&E Networks, 2021.

Maxim. "The U.S. Navy Has Reportedly Encountered Underwater UFOs That Move Incredibly Fast." July 29, 2022. https://www.maxim.com/news/us-navy-encountered-ufos-fast-underwater/.

Meessen, Auguste. "Apparitions and Miracles of the Sun." *International Forum in Porto "Science, Religion and Conscience"*, 2005, 199-222.

Mehta, Ravi, and Rui Zhu. "Blue or Red? Exploring the Effect of Color on Cognitive Task Performances." *Science* 323, no. 5918 (2009): 1226-1229.

"Memorandum from Dr. H. Marshall Chadwell to General Walter B. Smith, December 1952." Declassified CIA document, National Archives.

Michels, Jesse. "UFOs & Nukes: The Bizarre Truth Behind 'Jersey Drones'." *American Alchemy*. YouTube video, December 23, 2024. https://www.youtube.com/watch?v=fzvwBBSmWYA&t=1223s

———. "UFO Whistleblower: 'My Team Retrieved A UFO' (Jake Barber's Full Story)." *American Alchemy*. YouTube video, January 30, 2025. https://www.youtube.com/watch?v=dnnpyNuPdXs&t=168s.

———. "Steven Greer: 'UFO Secrets Are Held By A Global Cabal'." *American Alchemy*, YouTube video, April 10, 2025. https://www.youtube.com/watch?v=areO7Mej44E.

———. "Henry Kissinger & UFO Secrecy: The Dark Connection." *American Alchemy*. YouTube video, April 17, 2025. https://www.youtube.com/watch?v=JpfOZGY87c0.

———. "Presidential Advisor: 'I Directly Handled UFO Material' (Ft. Harald Malmgren)." *American Alchemy*. YouTube video, April 22, 2025. https://www.youtube.com/watch?v=09KP8XVf5nY.

Military.com. "UFO IN OUR BAFFLES, COMRADE CAPTAIN!" July 28, 2009. https://www.military.com/defensetech/2009/07/28/ufo-in-our-baffles-comrade-captain.

Mishlove, Jeffrey. "Poltergeist Agents with Barry Taff." Interview with Barry Taff. *Thinking Allowed*. YouTube Video, January 15, 2020. https://www.youtube.com/watch?v=V6F_h3dIh1M

Mitchell, Edgar. *The Way of the Explorer: An Apollo Astronaut's Journey Through the Material and Mystical Worlds*. New York: G.P. Putnam's Sons, 1996.

———. "Nature's Mind: The Quantum Hologram." National Institute for Discovery Science, 2011.

Moody, Raymond. *Making Sense of Nonsense: The Logical Bridge Between Science & Spirituality*. Woodbury, MN: Llewellyn Publications, 2020.

Morrison, Grant. "Pop Magik." In *Book of Lies: The Disinformation Guide to Magick and the Occult*, edited by Richard Metzger. New York: Disinformation Books, 2003.

———. Interview by Daniel Robert Epstein. *SuicideGirls*, February 27, 2005.

Morrison, Matt. "What Unsolved Mysteries Leaves Out About the Berkshires UFO Sightings." *Screenrant*, July 5, 2020.

Munsif Daily. "Indian Police Report UFO Sightings Over Nuclear Plants." March 27, 2024. https://munsifdaily.com/indian-police-report-ufo-sightings-over-nuclear-plants/.

"Mythological Motifs: Cosmic Egg Symbolism in Creation Stories." *Triple Moon Psychotherapy*. April 15, 2023. https://www.triplemoonpsychotherapy.com/archetypes-and-symbolism-myth-and-psyche/cosmic-egg-symbolism-dream-work-and-meanings.

Netflix. "Encounters." Documentary series. Released September 27, 2023.

NewsNation. "Ross Coulthart Reveals the Night that Convinced him to Investigate UFOs | Reality Check." *Reality Check with Ross Coulthart*. YouTube video, June 5, 2024. https://www.youtube.com/watch?v=VuCPbavls0U.

———. "'It is Pretty Strange:' Former Astronaut on Seeing Orbs | Morning in

America." YouTube video, December 30, 2024. https://www.youtube.com/watch?v=fIDOUWp-6VY.

———. "Whistleblower Reveals UAP Retrieval Program; Object Caught on Video." *Reality Check with Ross Coulthart*. YouTube video, January 19, 2025. https://www.youtube.com/watch?v=3dtA9w5ldHw

———. "UFO Whistleblower Jake Barber Would '100% Testify' Under Oath to Congress | Reality Check." *Reality Check with Ross Coulthart*. YouTube video, January 23, 2025. https://www.youtube.com/watch?v=t37-SKj4rtY&t=1370s

Newsweek. "'Egg UFO Retrieval' Video Underwhelms Alien Hunters." January 20, 2025. https://www.newsweek.com/egg-ufo-retrieval-video-underwhelms-alien-hunters-2017600.

Needham, Joseph. *Science and Civilisation in China, Vol. 2: History of Scientific Thought*. Cambridge: Cambridge University Press, 1956.

9News. "How an Unexplained UFO Encounter Tore a US Community Apart." *9News*, September 2, 2020.

Nolan, Garry. Interview by Lex Fridman. "UFOs and Aliens." *Lex Fridman Podcast*, Episode 367, July 12, 2023.

Ouyang, Xiu 欧阳修, and Song Qi 宋祁, comp. *New Book of Tang, Astronomical Records* (新唐书 天文志), c. 1044–1060. Reprint, Beijing: Zhonghua shuju, 1975.

Pasulka, Diana W. *American Cosmic: UFOs, Religion, Technology*. New York: Oxford University Press, 2019.

———. "Biblical UFOs & Occult NASA." Interview with Jesse Michels and Carl Nell, Hereticon Conference, 2024. YouTube video. https://www.youtube.com/watch?v=aa9Xx5wI8Rw

Peake, Anthony. *The Hidden Universe: An Investigation into Non-Human Intelligences*. London: Watkins Publishing, 2019.

Pendle, George. *Strange Angel: The Otherworldly Life of Rocket Scientist John Whiteside Parsons*. Orlando: Harcourt, 2005.

Penrose, Roger. *The Road to Reality: A Complete Guide to the Laws of the Universe*. London: Jonathan Cape, 2004.

"Pentagon Confirms Investigation into UFO Whistleblower Jake Barber's Allegations." *Liberation Times*, February 22, 2025. https://www.liberationtimes.com/home/pentagon-confirms-investigation-into-ufo-whistleblower-jake-barbers-allegations.

Persinger, Michael A. "The Tectonic Strain Theory as an Explanation for UFO Phenomena: A Non-Technical Review of the Research, 1970–1990." *Journal of UFO Studies* 2 (1990): 105–137.

———., and Gyslaine F. Lafrenière. *Space-Time Transients and Unusual Events*. Chicago: Nelson-Hall, 1977.

Pflock, Karl T. "Roswell in Perspective." Fund for UFO Research, 1994.

Wang, Hengxiu 王恒修, and Zhang Cheng 张诚. *Pinghu County Chronicles, Records of Anomalies* (平湖县志), 1790.

"PRC: Scientists Identify Xinjiang UFO as Plasma Fireball." Central Intelligence Agency (FOIA Reading Room), Document #0005516241. April 20, 1988.

"Preliminary Assessment: Unidentified Aerial Phenomena." Washington, DC: Office of the Director of National Intelligence, June 25, 2021.

Rabeyron, Thomas. "When the Truth Is Out There: Counseling People Who Report Anomalous Experiences." *Frontiers in Psychology* 12 (2022). doi:10.3389/fpsyg.2021.693707.

———., and Tianna Loose. "Anomalous Experiences, Trauma, and Symbolization Processes at the Frontiers between Psychoanalysis and Cognitive Neurosciences." *Frontiers in Psychology* 6 (2015). https://pmc.ncbi.nlm.nih.gov/articles/PMC4685320/. doi:10.3389/fpsyg.2015.01926.

Ramirez, John. Interview by UAP Files Podcast. "UFOs, UAPs & 2027: Former CIA Agent John Ramirez Tells All." YouTube video, March 16, 2024. https://www.youtube.com/watch?v=v6wGLH1uSOo.

Randles, Jenny. *UFO Reality: A Critical Look at the Physical Evidence*. London: Robert Hale, 1983.

Randolph, Paschal Beverly. *The Mysteries of Eulis*. Privately published, 1874.

Reagan, Ronald. "Address to the United Nations General Assembly." Speech, New York, NY, September 21, 1987.

Redfern, Nick. *The UFO Encyclopedia: The Phenomenon from the Beginning*. Detroit: Visible Ink Press, 2018.

"Retired USAF Captain Recalls UFO Encounter, Says Aliens Turned Off Nuclear Warheads." *Yahoo News*, November 27, 2024.

Richet, Charles. *Thirty Years of Psychical Research*. New York: Macmillan, 1923.

Ring, Kenneth. *The Omega Project: Near-Death Experiences, UFO Encounters, and Mind at Large*. New York: William Morrow & Co., 1992.

Roerich, Nicholas. *Altai-Himalaya: A Travel Diary*. New York: Nicholas Roerich Museum, 2017.

Rogo, D. Scott. *The Haunted Universe*. New York: Signet, 1979.

Roll, William G. "Poltergeists, Electromagnetism and Consciousness." *Journal of Scientific Exploration* 17, no. 1 (2003): 75–86.

Rojcewicz, Peter M. "The Extraordinary Encounter Continuum Hypothesis and Its Implications for the Study of Belief Materials." *Folklore Forum* 19, no. 2 (1986): 131–152.

Rosen, David. *The Tao of Jung: The Way of Integrity*. New York: Penguin Putnam, 1996.

Rutledge, Harley D. 1981. *Project Identification: The First Scientific Study of UFO Phenomena*. Englewood Cliffs, NJ: Prentice-Hall.

Rux, Bruce. *Architects of the Underworld: Unriddling Atlantis, Anomalies of Mars, and the Mystery of the Sphinx*. Berkeley: Frog Books, 1996.

Sagan, Carl. *Broca's Brain: Reflections on the Romance of Science.* New York: Random House, 1979.

———. *Pale Blue Dot: A Vision of the Human Future in Space.* New York: Random House, 1994.

Saha, Pritam. "India Reports UFO Sightings? Policeman Spots Mysterious Objects Zooming Above Nuclear Plant." *Republic World,* March 27, 2024. https://www.republicworld.com/india/india-reports-ufo-sightings-police man-spots-mysterious-objects-zooming-above-nuclear-plant.

Salas, Robert. "*UFOs: Investigating the Unknown.*" Interview with *National Geographic,* 2023.

Santa, Scott. "Drive-in Theater UFO Encounter at Cuyahoga Falls, Ohio." *AP Magazine,* February 2021.

Schectman, Joel, and Aruna Viswanatha. "The Pentagon Disinformation That Fueled America's UFO Mythology." *Wall Street Journal,* June 6, 2025. https://www.wsj.com/politics/national-security/ufo-us-disinformation-45376f7e.

Schindele, David D. *It Never Happened, Volume 1: U.S. Air Force UFO Cover-up Revealed.* EdgarRock Publishing, 2017.

Schwartz, Benjamin. *The World of Thought in Ancient China.* Cambridge: Harvard University Press, 1985.

Scrivner, Coltan, John A. Johnson, Jens Kjeldgaard-Christiansen, and Mathias Clasen. "Pandemic Practice: Horror Fans and Morbidly Curious Individuals Are More Psychologically Resilient During the COVID-19 Pandemic." *Personality and Individual Differences* 168 (2021): 110397. https://doi.org/10.1016/j.paid.2020.110397.

Shanghai Observer. "The Astronomer Who Calmed China's UFO Craze." *Sixth Tone,* May 20, 2023.

Shanghai Songjiang Prefecture Chronicles Sequel (上海松江府续志), 1885.

Shen, Heyong. "C.G. Jung and China: A Continued Dialogue." *Jung Journal: Culture & Psyche* 3, no. 2 (2009): 5–14.

Shen, Kuo 沈括. *Dream Pool Essays* (梦溪笔谈), c. 1088. Punctuated by Hu Daojing 胡道静. Shanghai: Shanghai guji chubanshe, 1987.

Shi, Jianwu 施肩吾. *Zhong Lü Chuandao Ji* (钟吕传道记). Edited by Wang Tinggui 王庭珪, c. 1143. Translated by Jane Huang. In *Cultivating the Energy of Life.* Boston: Shambhala, 1998.

Shklovskii, I. S., and Carl Sagan. *Intelligent Life in the Universe.* San Francisco: Holden-Day, 1966.

Shuster, Julie. "My Father Saw the Bodies: Chasing the Truth About Roswell." SBS, July 23, 2021. https://www.sbs.com.au/whats-on/article/my-father-saw-the-bodies-chasing-the-truth-about-roswell/thp111yiy

Smith, Anna Nicole. Interview with *FHM Magazine,* 2004.

Somé, Malidoma Patrice. *Of Water and the Spirit: Ritual, Magic, and Initiation in the Life of an African Shaman.* New York: Penguin Books, 1995.

Songzi County Chronicles (松滋县志), c. 1880.

States, Bert O. "Dreaming and Storytelling." *Critical Inquiry* 20, no. 1 (1993): 158–176.

Stollznow, Karen. "Sleeping with the Entity: Sexual Assaults by Incubi." *Skeptical Inquirer* 36, no. 3 (2012): 46–49.

Strassberg, Richard E. *A Chinese Bestiary: Strange Creatures from the Guideways Through Mountains and Seas*. University of California Press, 2002.

Struck, Peter T. *Birth of the Symbol: Ancient Readers at the Limits of Their Texts*. Princeton: Princeton University Press, 2004.

Solomon, Libby. "No Place to Run: Loch Raven Reservoir's Forgotten UFO, 60 Years Later." *The Baltimore Sun*, October 22, 2018. https://www.baltimoresun.com/2018/10/22/no-place-to-run-loch-raven-reservoirs-forgotten-ufo-60-years-later/.

Sprague, Ryan. "A Mass UFO Sighting at a Drive-In Theater Still Amazes." *Point of Contact* (Medium), July 7, 2021.

Stephen, Leslie. "The Skepticism of Believers." In *An Agnostic's Apology and Other Essays*, 226–275. London: Smith, Elder & Co., 1893.

Stevens, Wendelle C., and Paul Dong. *UFOs Over Modern China*. Tucson, AZ: UFO Photo Archives, 1983.

Strieber, Whitley. *Communion: A True Story*. New York: Beech Tree Books, 1987.

———. *Transformation: The Breakthrough*. New York: William Morrow, 1988.

Sun, Hang, and Eunyoung Kim. "Archetype Symbols and Altered Consciousness: A Study of Shamanic Rituals in the Context of Jungian Psychology." *Frontiers in Psychology* (May 9, 2024).

Suzuki, Shunryu. *Zen Mind, Beginner's Mind*. Boston: Shambhala, 1970.

Swedenborg, Emanuel. *Heaven and Hell*. Translated by George F. Dole. West Chester, PA: Swedenborg Foundation, 2000.

Symbol Sage. "The Power of Eggs in Folklore." October 15, 2024. https://symbolsage.com/power-of-eggs-in-folklore/.

Taff, Barry. *Aliens Above, Ghosts Below: Explorations of the Unknown*. Los Angeles: Cosmic Pantheon Press, 2014.

Taiwan UFOlogy Society (台灣飛碟學會). https://ufo.ikh.tw/

Taiwan UFO News Database (台灣飛碟新聞資料庫). https://ikh.tw/ufomag/

Talbot, Michael. *The Holographic Universe: The Revolutionary Theory of Reality*. New York: Harper Perennial, 2011.

Teodorani, Massimo. "The Intelligent Plasma Hypothesis." Dr. Massimo Teodorani (blog), June 8, 2019.

"The Conundrum of The Phenomenon | Sekret Machines Vol. 3 [WAR] with Jim Semivan & Peter Levenda." Interview. YouTube video, May 29, 2025. https://www.youtube.com/watch?v=hQ4w-3IC-Zs

The Express. "Area 51 Stored Egg-Shaped, SUV-Sized UFO in the 1980s, Claims Whistleblower." December 12, 2023. https://www.express.co.uk/news/

weird/1844931/area-51-egg-shaped-ufo-1980s-whistleblower.

"The Fayetteville, North Carolina Encounter, January 8, 2007." *UFO Casebook*, 2008.

"The Gateway Process." Declassified CIA document, approved for release 2003/09/10, CIA-RDP96-00788R001700210016-5.

"The Marian Apparitions at Zeitoun with Travis Dumsday." Interview by Jeffrey Mishlove. *New Thinking Allowed*. YouTube video, November 17, 2024. https://www.youtube.com/watch?v=wtfRmbZJ_Qo.

"The Power of the Placebo Effect." *Harvard Health*, July 22, 2019. https://www.health.harvard.edu/newsletter_article/the-power-of-the-placebo-effect.

The Truth About Aliens and UFOs (外星人UFO真相). https://www.etufo.org.

"The US Military Has Logged Many UFO Encounters Near Nuclear Facilities." *History*, November 17, 2022.

Thibodeau, Paul H., and Lera Boroditsky. "Metaphors We Think With: The Role of Metaphor in Reasoning." *PLoS ONE* 6, no. 2 (2011): e16782. https://doi.org/10.1371/journal.pone.0016782.

Thompson, Malcolm. "On UFOlogy with Chinese Characteristics and the Fate of Chinese Socialism." *Made in China Journal*, October 19, 2020.

Tongling County Chronicles of Anhui (安徽铜陵县志), 1757.

Tucker, Jim B. *Life Before Life: A Scientific Investigation of Children's Memories of Previous Lives*. New York: St. Martin's Press, 2005.

Tuotuo 脱脱 et al., comp. *History of Song, Astronomical Records* (宋史天文志), 1345. Reprint, Beijing: Zhonghua shuju, 1977.

Twain, Mark. "Mental Telegraphy." 1891. In *The Complete Essays of Mark Twain*, edited by Charles Neider. Cambridge, MA: Da Capo Press, 2000.

Tyler, Royall. *Japanese Tales*. Pantheon Books, 1987.

"UFO Debate Invades Politicians' Space." *Reuters*, December 21, 2007. https://www.reuters.com/article/lifestyle/ufo-debate-invades-politicians-space-idUSN21257574/.reuters

"UFO Phenomenon in China Analyzed." *China Report: Science and Technology*, JPRS 77236, no. 79, pp. 1–5. Central Intelligence Agency (FOIA Reading Room), Document #C00174701. January 26, 1981.

"UFO Sighting Over Nuclear Power Plant in India Baffles Locals." *Geo TV*, March 28, 2024.

United Nations. "Letter from Gordon Cooper to United Nations, 1978." In *UFOs: Generals, Pilots, and Government Officials Go on the Record*, edited by Leslie Kean, 65–67. New York: Crown Publishing, 2010.

Urushibara, Yuki. "Autobiographical Interlude." In *Mushishi*, vol. 1. Tokyo: Kodansha, 1999, pp. 176–178.

U.S. Department of Defense. "Anomalous Acute and Subacute Field Effects on Human and Biological Tissues." Defense Intelligence Agency, March 2010.

Vallée, Jacques. *Passport to Magonia: From Folklore to Flying Saucers.* Chicago: Henry Regnery Company, 1969.

———. *Messengers of Deception: UFO Contacts and Cults.* Berkeley: And/Or Press, 1979.

———. *Confrontations: A Scientist's Search for Alien Contact.* New York: Ballantine Books, 1990.

van Lankveld, Jacques J.D.M., et al. "Altered States of Consciousness Are Related to Higher Sexual Responsiveness in Women, and to a Lesser Extent in Men." *Journal of Sex & Marital Therapy* 42, no. 4 (2016): 313–324.

Wang, Guan 王瓘. *Guang Huangdi Benxing Ji* (广黄帝本行记), 881.

"Watching the Skies in Japan: Mishima Yukio and Other UFO Enthusiasts." Nippon.com, July 1, 2023.

Watson, Nigel. *Captured by Aliens? A History and Analysis of American Abduction Claims.* Jefferson: McFarland, 2020.

Weinberger, Sharon. *The Imagineers of War: The Untold Story of DARPA.* New York: Knopf, 2017.

Wheeler, John Archibald. "Law Without Law." In *Quantum Theory and Measurement*, edited by John Archibald Wheeler and Wojciech Hubert Zurek, 182–213. Princeton: Princeton University Press, 1983.

———. "Information, Physics, Quantum: The Search for Links." In *Complexity, Entropy, and the Physics of Information*, edited by Wojciech H. Zurek, 3–28. Redwood City, CA: Addison-Wesley, 1990.

"Why Do UFO Sightings Keep Happening Near Nuclear Sites?" *VICE*, August 9, 2024. https://www.vice.com/en/article/why-do-ufo-sightings-keep-happening-near-nuclear-sites/.

Wilhelm, Richard, trans. *The Secret of the Golden Flower: A Chinese Book of Life.* With commentary by C.G. Jung. English translation by Cary F. Baynes. London: Routledge & Kegan Paul, 1962. Originally published in German in 1929.

———., trans. *The I Ching or Book of Changes.* With foreword by C.G. Jung. English translation by Cary F. Baynes. Princeton: Princeton University Press, 1950.

Wilson, Colin. *The Occult: A History.* London: Hodder & Stoughton, 1971.

Winkelman, Michael. "Shamanism as the Original Neurotheology." *Zygon* 39, no. 1 (March 2004): 193–217.

Wright, Kevin. "Using the Wall Street Journal, the Pentagon is Gaslighting the Public on UFOs—Again." *New Paradigm Institute*, June 7, 2025. https://newparadigminstitute.org/learn/library/using-the-wall-street-journal-the-pentagon-is-gaslighting-the-public-on-ufos-again/.

Wu, Youru 吴友如. "Red Flame in Flight (赤焰腾空)." *Dianshizhai Pictorial* (点石斋画报), 1892.

Xunzi. *Xunzi: The Complete Text.* Translated by Eric L. Hutton. Princeton: Princeton University Press, 2014.

Yang, Shao-hua. "Ancient Aliens in China: The Sanxingdui Controversy and Alternative Archaeology." *Asian Anthropology* 19, no. 1 (2020): 54–71.

Yao, Tongshou 姚桐壽. Lejiao siyu (乐郊私语), c. 1363. In *Shuo fu* (说郛). Reprint, Shanghai: Shanghai guji chubanshe, 1988.

Zaoqiang County Chronicles of Hebei (河北枣强县志), 1931.

Zha/Cha, Leping, and Lin Hongjing. "Preliminary Survey of Unidentified Aerial Phenomena in China." Central Intelligence Agency (FOIA Reading Room), Document Number 0005516652. January 26, 1981. https://www.cia.gov/readingroom/document/0005516652

Zhenhai County Chronicles, Records of Anomalies (镇海县志 祥异志), 1879.

Zhuangzi. Translated by Burton Watson. New York: Columbia University Press, 2013.

ACKNOWLEDGMENTS

Everything is born from relationships, and this is certainly true in regard to this book which would not exist without certain people, books, places in the woods, or moments at dawn.

First off, a special thanks to 陈玉芬, 尚秉祺, 徐继欣, John Alleman, Bil Brown, Frank Xavier Quickert, and Jeffrey Skinner. They taught us to love ideas not as final truths but as art objects in an art gallery of invisible things.

Thank you as well to our parents who taught us light—尚秀华, Shirley St. Pierre, 于兆太, Johnny Lee Branscum, Diana Feger, and Edward Lawson—and the dear friends who gave us valuable advice, inspiration, and love: 韩世亮, 尚秀萍, 张晶鹏, 苑蔚, 邵梦, 周佩蓉, Rajwan Alshareefy, Eric Clark, Carri Cleaveland, Chauna Craig, Patrick Craig, Lauren Elise Daniels, Geneve Flynn, Vanessa Fogg, Ai Jiang, Jialei Jiang, Kristy Park Kulski, Danning Liang, Fang-Yu Liao, Zahraa Mubarak, Lee Murray, Xueting C. Ni, Gian Pagnucci, Frances Pai, Xiubo Cui Pearce, Curt Porter, T Stacy Reynolds, Bob Rickard, Eric Roper, Rosemary Thorne, Dan Weinstein, Berry Xu, and all the wonderful people of the HWA.

Additionally, we are indebted to the students we've been lucky enough to teach, who in the process have taught us so much in return.

Finally, a grateful thank you to the following journals and all the lovely, hardworking people behind them for publishing some of the pieces in this book: *Black & Grey Magazine, Copper Nickel, Lunch Ticket, New England Review, Passages North,* and *Strange Horizons-Samovar.*

ABOUT THE AUTHORS

Yi Izzy Yu works, writes, and cavorts in the weird wilds of Pennsylvania. A former professor at both Chinese and American universities, she now works as a translator and cultural consultant. She is the co-translator of the acclaimed *The Shadow Book of Ji Yun*, and her fiction, nonfiction, and literary translations have appeared in magazines and anthologies ranging from *New England Review* and *Strange Horizons-Samovar* to *Unquiet Spirits: Essays by Asian Women in Horror* and *Silk & Sinew: A Collection of Folk Horror from the Asian Diaspora*. She was named a finalist for the 2024 Ignyte Award in Nonfiction and for the 2020 Gabriel García Márquez "Gabo" Award for Literature in Translation.

John Yu Branscum has published books with Sarabande Books, Argus House Press, and Empress Wu Books, and short form work in magazines ranging from *Cincinnati Review* to *Apex Magazine*. He is a recipient of the Ursula Le Guin Award for Imaginative Literature, the Sarah Bruckheimer Award for Literature, and the Argus House Press Award for Poetry. He enjoys family rave nights, durian fruit, and lucid dream vacations. Currently, he is in the midst of a long-term performance art project that involves working as a professor of comparative literature, creative writing, and consciousness studies at Indiana University of Pennsylvania, and as editor for the fashion and literature magazine *Black & Grey*.

ALSO BY YI IZZY YU AND JOHN YU BRANSCUM

ZHIGUAI

Chinese True Tales of the Paranormal and Glitches in the Matrix

Edited and Translated by

YI IZZY YU
JOHN YU BRANSCUM

www.ingramcontent.com/pod-product-compliance
Lightning Source LLC
Chambersburg PA
CBHW030516080526
44586CB00011B/211